On Eagles' Wings:
The King James Bible Turns 400

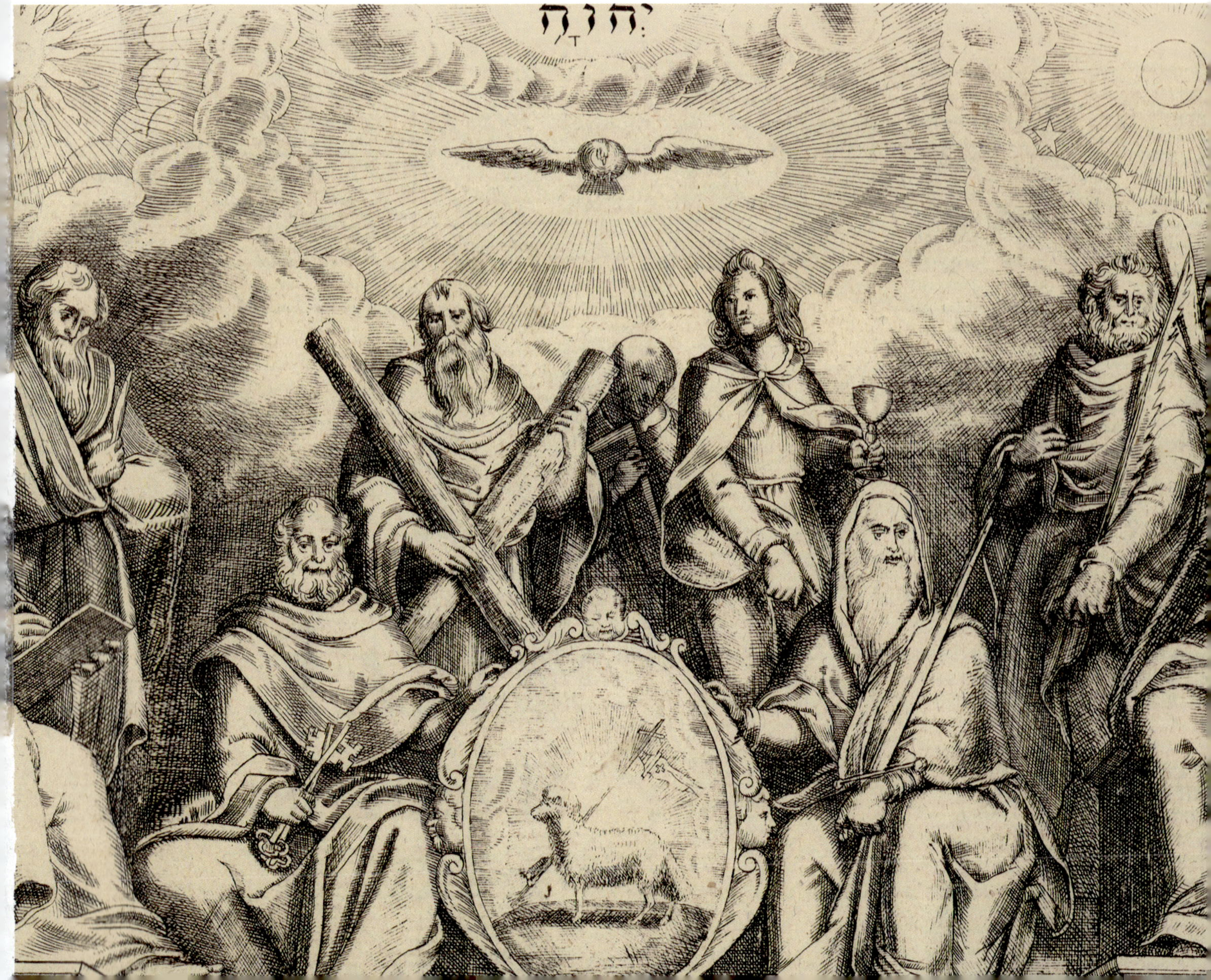

On Eagles' Wings:
The King James Bible Turns 400

Liana Lupas

FEATURING THE ART OF MAKOTO FUJIMURA

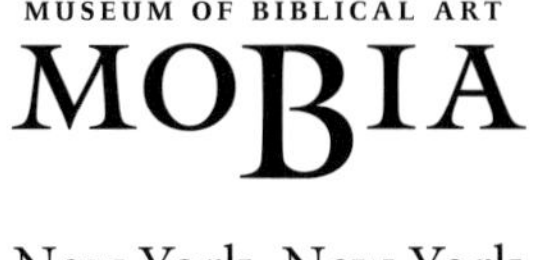

MUSEUM OF BIBLICAL ART
MOBIA
New York, New York

Display and conservation of the Rare Bible Collection @ MOBIA is made possible, in part, by the generous support of the American Bible Society.

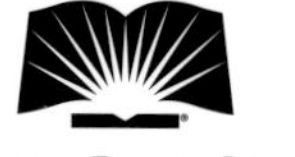

AMERICAN BIBLE SOCIETY

ISBN 0-9777839-8-7

Edited by Patricia C. Pongracz, Ph.D., Director of Curatorial Affairs, MOBIA

Photography of the Rare Bible Collection @ MOBIA by Gina Fuentes Walker

Graphic Design by Kara Van Woerden

PUBLISHED ON THE OCCASION OF THE EXHIBITION
ON EAGLES' WINGS: THE KING JAMES BIBLE TURNS 400
PRESENTED AT MOBIA
JULY 8, 2011 THROUGH OCTOBER 16, 2011

Major support for MOBIA's exhibitions and programs has been provided by the American Bible Society and by Howard and Roberta Ahmanson. This program is supported, in part, by public funds from the New York City Department of Cultural Affairs, in partnership with the City Council and with public funds from the New York State Council on the Arts, celebrating 50 years of building strong, creative communities in New York's 62 counties.

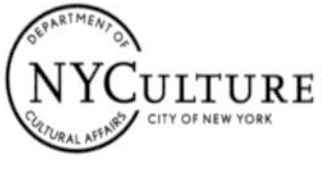 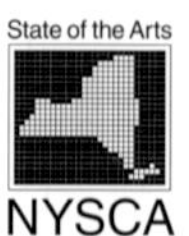

Reproductions of the artworks from *The Four Holy Gospels* are generously provided by Makoto Fujimara and licensed by Crossway, Wheaton, Illinois.

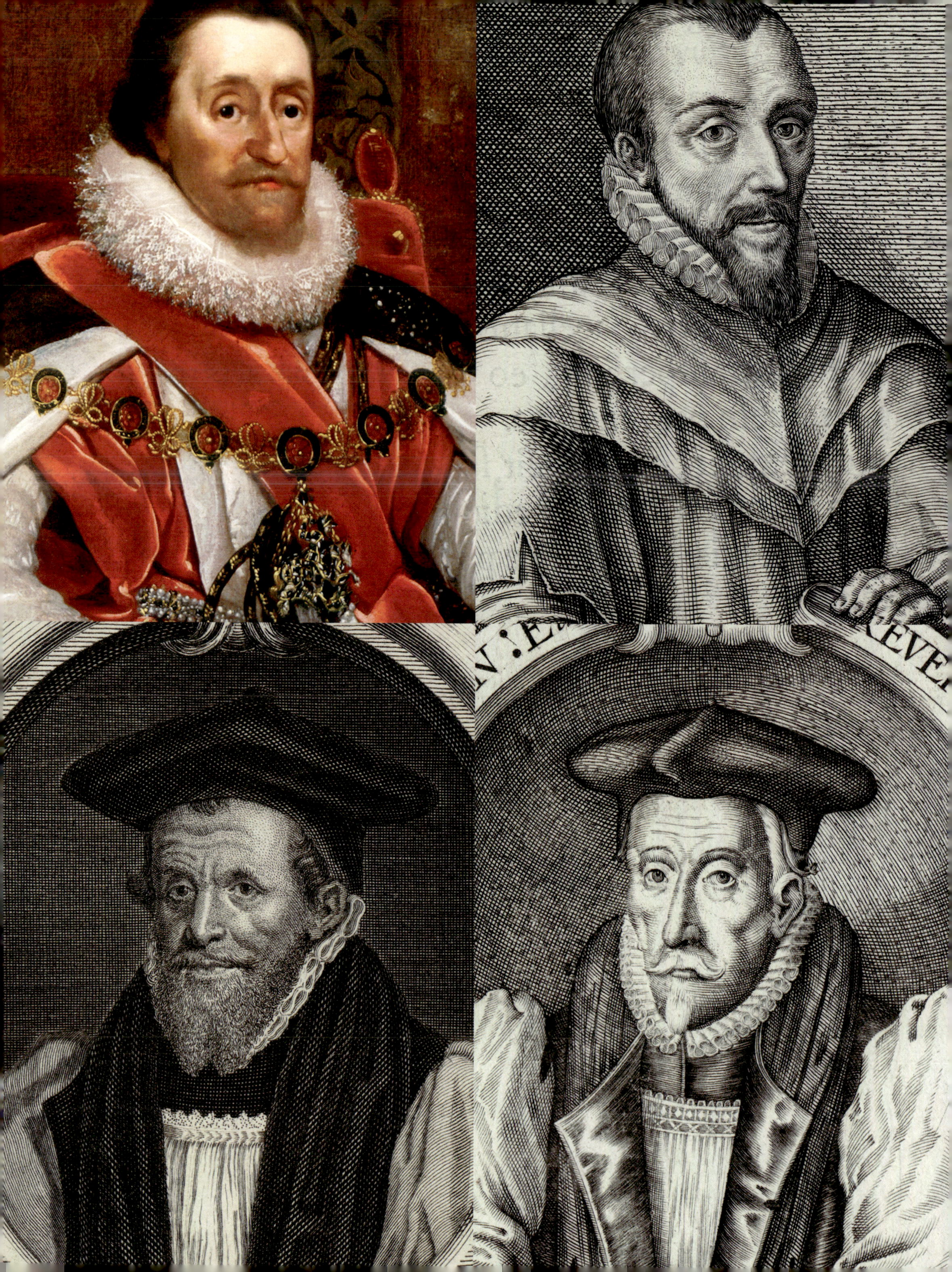

Contents

9   FOREWORD
Ena Heller, Ph.D., Executive Director, MOBIA

11   AUTHOR'S ACKNOWLEDGEMENTS
Liana Lupas, Ph.D., Curator, Rare Bible Collection @ MOBIA

13   PREFACE

15   I. THE ENGLISH BIBLE BEFORE KING JAMES

45   II. BIRTH OF A MASTERPIECE

67   III. EARLY EDITIONS OF THE KING JAMES BIBLE (1611–1800)

107   IV. THE KING JAMES BIBLE IN AMERICA (1782–1800)

123   V. THE BIBLE SOCIETY MOVEMENT (1804–1854)

133   VI. MODERN AND CONTEMPORARY EDITIONS (1800–2005)

157   VII. CELEBRATING THE KING JAMES BIBLE IN 2011
Adrianne Rubin, Ph.D., Assistant Curator and Registrar, MOBIA

163   CHECKLIST

166   LIST OF ILLUSTRATIONS

167   BIBLIOGRAPHY

On Eagles' Wings: The King James Bible Turns 400 is an exhibition about milestones. The most obvious one, of course, is the historical event it celebrates: the 400th anniversary of the King James Bible. First printed in 1611 the King James remains the most influential Bible in the English language, and arguably the single most influential book for the evolution of the English language and the history of literature in English. For MOBIA, the exhibition also marks three institutional firsts—institutional milestones. One derives from the fact that no one exhibition can hope to tell the complete story of the King James, so *On Eagles' Wings* (which outlines the creation, publication and dissemination of this monumental translation) is the beginning of a year-long program of exhibitions that will add to the narrative by tracing the impact of the King James on discrete chapters of biblical history: American Family Bibles (fall 2011) and Bibles printed especially for soldiers (spring 2012).

The second milestone marks the first time when so many volumes (52 to be exact) from the Rare Bible Collection @ MOBIA will be on view. This extraordinary collection, built by the American Bible Society since 1817 and lent to MOBIA in 2010 so it can be actively conserved and shared with a wider public, is the largest collection of printed Bibles in the Western hemisphere—and one of the best kept secrets in New York. We hope that *On Eagles' Wings* will contribute greatly to making this remarkable collection be more broadly appreciated.

The third milestone brings MOBIA's very mission into sharp focus by connecting the history of the King James Bible with its most recent artistic legacy, the Four Gospel project by New York artist Makoto Fujimura. Fujimura's paintings, created for a 21st century commemorative edition of the Gospels, published by Crossway, Wheaton, IL, renew a long—and some would say lost—tradition of illuminated Bibles, and translate the practice of illumination into a contemporary idiom. The juxtaposition of old and new, written and pictorial underscores our definition of biblical art as on-going, multi-faceted, and multi-disciplinary.

Since the author of this catalog, Dr. Liana Lupas, acknowledged the whole team who helped produce this book and organize the exhibition it accompanies, I will limit my acknowledgements here to Dr. Lupas herself, and will simply say that our efforts to publicize and publish the Rare Bible Collection @ MOBIA would not be in the least successful were it not for Dr. Lupas's scholarship, passion, and tireless dedication. Her extraordinary knowledge and ability to make even the most esoteric materials seem exciting and even fun are unparalleled. I hope that this catalog, as well as the exhibition, provides a history in which all our visitors will discover something new.

Ena Heller, Ph.D.
Executive Director

Acknowledgements

My gratitude goes to many colleagues and friends who have assisted me while I was in the throes of preparing this Catalog: to Dr. Ena Heller, Executive Director of MOBIA, for supporting the project and writing the Foreword; to Dr. Patricia Pongracz, Director of Curatorial Affairs, for her inexhaustible patience and countless suggestions; to Dr. Adrianne Rubin, Assistant Curator and Registrar, for reading the final draft and making many editorial comments; to Kate Williamson, Curatorial Assistant, for liaising with the British institutions that kindly let us use images from their collections and coping with my technological incompetence; to Clare Manias, Conservator, for rescuing printed books that seemed beyond repair; and to Dean Ebben, Artist and Preparator and Lead Art Handler, for designing the exhibition and assisting our photographer, Gina Fuentes Walker, over the many days it took to photograph the works on display.

I also wish to thank the leadership and staff of the American Bible Society, who hired me more than 20 years ago and offered me the chance to care for their priceless Scripture Collection. Learning about the Bibles entrusted to me and sharing with others my love for them has been a blessing and a daily joy.

Last, but by no means least, I would like to thank Dr. David G. Burke, Dean Emeritus of the Eugene A. Nida Institute for Biblical Scholarship, for reading my manuscript and helping me correct an untold number of factual and typographical errors.

Liana Lupas, Ph.D.
Curator, Rare Bible Collection @ MOBIA

"Ye have seen what I did unto the Egyptians, and how I bare you on eagles' wings, and brought you unto myself."

Exodus 19:4

On Eagles' Wings

Produced by a committee of fifty-odd scholars who labored for about seven years at the special commandment of James I, the Bible known today as the King James Version appears forever young as it turns 400. It originated in the King's desire to bring religious unity to his realm and was conceived as a revision of the English Bible published during the reign of Queen Elizabeth. The King's team used the Hebrew and Greek texts, the previous English versions, and a variety of other translations and commentaries. Their aim was to produce a faithful rendition of the Hebrew and Greek originals and provide a translation appropriate for liturgical reading in churches while also avoiding theological disputes. To say this translation has passed the test of time with flying colors would be a serious understatement. These scholars created the most influential English Bible and a model for future translations in thousands of languages. Practically forgotten as individuals and almost hidden behind the paramount significance of the text they had crafted, they earned a place among the great masters of English literary prose almost by accident.

No exhibition can do full justice to the King James Bible. The purpose of the present one is to tell the story of this iconic translation from the moment of its conception in January 1604 to its last scholarly revision in 2005 by displaying printed editions drawn from the Rare Bible Collection @ MOBIA and facsimile copies of portraits and documents preserved in British collections. Special emphasis is placed on the history of the text and its most beautifully printed and illustrated editions.

I. The English Bible before King James

Several English translations of the Bible were in use when James VI of Scotland became James I of England and none of them was acceptable to all his subjects. Elizabeth's Bishops had launched in 1568 an official translation that never became popular, the Puritan exiles had issued in Geneva in 1560 a version that sold many copies in England, but was rejected by the clergy, and the Catholic exiles had published in Rheims in 1582 their own New Testament based on the Vulgate and heavily annotated. The history of the Bible in English started long before Elizabeth's accession with John Wyclif in the 1380s and William Tyndale, Miles Coverdale, and John Rogers in the 1520s and 1530s. As new translations and fresh revisions continued to be printed, an English thesaurus of biblical phrases was developed amid controversies and polemics. The translators of the King James Bible were the beneficiaries of this rich tradition and inherited from their predecessors the building blocks of English biblical phraseology and diction. They enjoyed royal patronage and secure positions within the higher clergy and the universities while almost all the translators before them had faced rejection and persecution and several died violent deaths. Wyclif was condemned posthumously, Tyndale and Rogers were burned at the stake, Coverdale had to flee England three times, and all the scholars who worked on the Geneva and the Rheims-Douay versions were exiles.

The translators commissioned by King James crafted an English Bible that remained the standard Protestant version in both Britain and America for more than 300 years. As indicated in the title of the 1611 folio, their success was connected to their creative use of "former translations" and cannot be dissociated from the early history of the Bible in English.

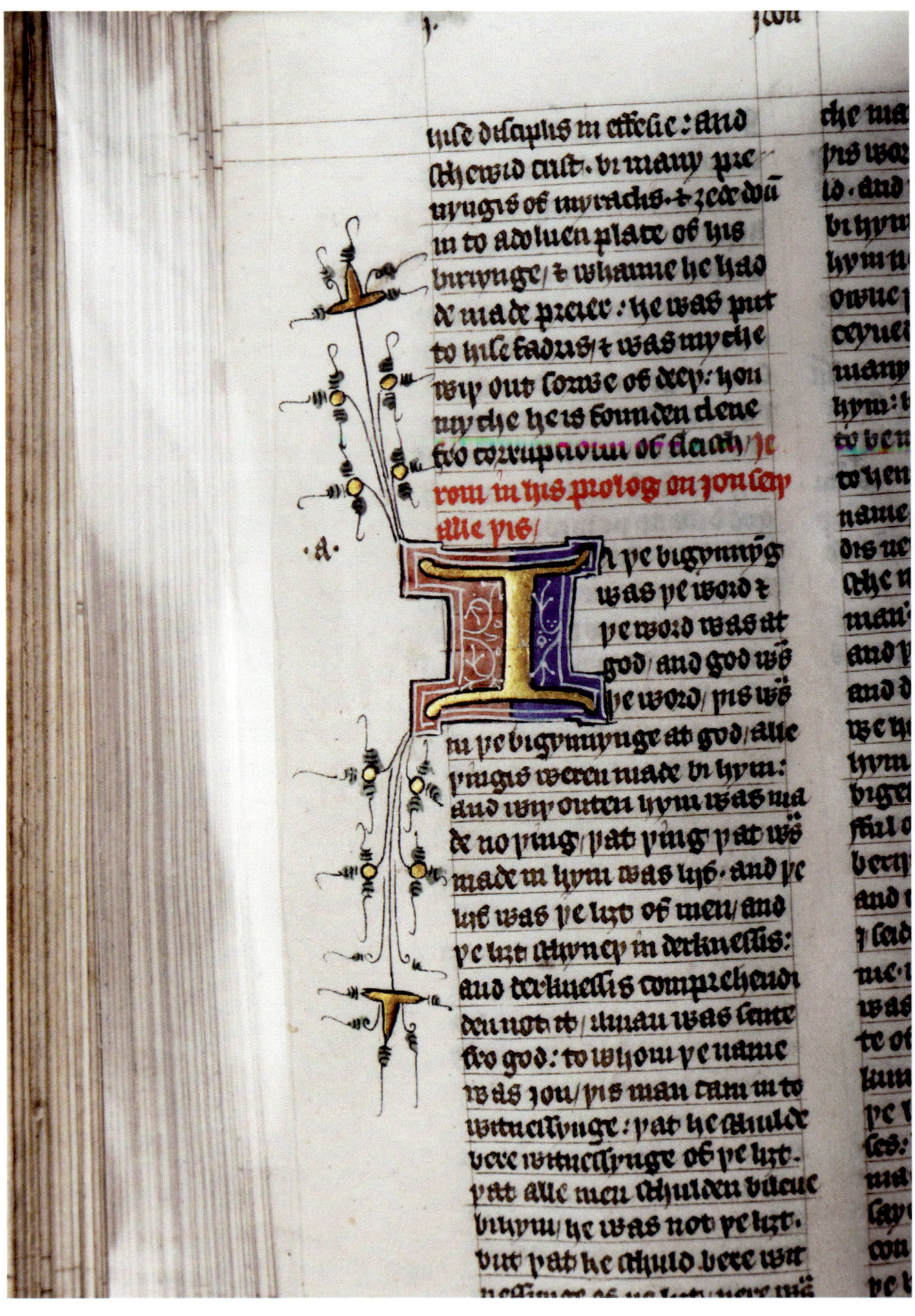

1. New Testament

MANUSCRIPT ON VELLUM, C. 1440

[2], 230, [2]; 234 ff. 185 x 130 mm.

The first English translation of the entire Bible dates from the 1380s and was ascribed to the Oxford scholar and theologian John Wyclif (or Wycliffe, *c.* 1330–1384). While it is unlikely that Wyclif had any part in the actual process of translating, there is no doubt that the translators were his followers and disciples. Their work survives in some 250 manuscripts, of which 20 have the complete Bible and about 100, the New Testament. The remaining group consists of some 50 manuscripts of the Gospels or the Epistles and some 70 that have various combinations of biblical books and fragments. The number of manuscripts preserving other literary texts in English is considerably lower: there are 180 surviving copies of the so-called "Brut Chronicle of England" and only 64 of Chaucer's *Canterbury Tales*.[1]

1. De Hamel 2001: 168, 180

The manuscripts of the Wycliffite Bible do not derive from a single archetype, but represent two distinct stages of the text: a literal translation of the Latin Vulgate that reads almost like a collection of glosses, and a more fluent and idiomatic version, much closer to modern English diction. The only critical edition of the complete text, prepared by Josiah Forshall and Sir Frederic Madden in 1850, prints the two versions in parallel columns with an exhaustive critical apparatus based on 150 manuscripts. The more stilted version predates the more readable one and was done in Oxford sometime between 1380 and 1384. According to a note included in two of the earliest Wycliffite manuscripts, the Old Testament from Genesis to Baruch 3:20 was translated by Nicholas of Hereford (d. *c.* 1420), a theologian who was ordained in 1370, received a doctorate from Oxford in 1382, was excommunicated for heresy the same year, lost his appeal in Rome, and was jailed there for three years. These unfortunate circumstances may explain why he stopped working on the translation abruptly in the middle of Baruch. The names of the translators who completed the early version remain unknown.

Most surviving manuscripts have the later, revised, version of the Wycliffite text, dating from about 1388. At least one copyist ascribes it to a certain "J," identified by Forshall and Madden as John Purvey (*c.* 1354–*c.* 1421), Wyclif's secretary during his last year. Other scholars, including David Daniell,[2] believe that "J" stands for John Trevisa (1342–1402), who is mentioned as a Bible translator by Miles Smith in the Preface to the King James Bible. To make things even more complicated, it appears that readings from both versions of the Wycliffite Bible are combined in some manuscripts.

2. Daniell 2003: 91-95

John Wyclif was a brilliant professor of scholastics as well as a precursor of the Reformation. He had extremely influential patrons, such as John of Gaunt, Richard II's uncle, and Joan of Kent, the King's mother, who protected him when he was suspected of heresy in 1377 and 1378. His unorthodox views on the doctrine of transubstantiation forced him to retire from Oxford in 1380, but he was allowed to spend his last years in Lutterworth, where he wrote some 57 works in Latin. He was condemned posthumously at the Council of Constance in 1415, when Jan Hus was also found guilty and was burned at the stake. The persecution against Wyclif's disciples started in the 1370s, but became far more intense after his death. In 1407–08 Archbishop Thomas Arundel convened at Oxford a Provincial Council and in 1409 the Council adopted a Constitution that made translating the Bible into English or reading an English translation of the Bible a capital crime unless expressly allowed by a bishop. John Wyclif was mentioned by name in the document. Arundel's Constitution was used to track down the Lollards, a large group of dissenters who had adopted Wyclif's doctrines and were using and spreading the Wycliffite Bibles. Extant records of heresy trials show that countless Lollards were convicted for possessing Wycliffite Bibles. Five were burned in London in 1496 with their manuscripts tied around their necks.[3]

With almost no exception, the 250 surviving Bible manuscripts are expensive artifacts, copied on vellum rather than paper and embellished with elaborate initials, some in gold. They have never been the property of poor preachers. In fact, one of them can be traced back to King Henry VI (1422–71), another one was signed by the future Richard III while he was still Duke of Gloucester (prior to 1483), and a third one has probably belonged to Thomas of Woodstock, first Duke of Gloucester (1355–1397). They were used for private devotion in conjunction with the Latin text read aloud during the liturgy. The margins of many pages have small letters from *a* to *g* that help the reader connect the English translation with the Latin lesson.[4]

By the time Arundel's Oxford Constitution ceased to be enforced, in 1529, the Wycliffite Bible had ceased to be copied, Tyndale had already published his translation of the New Testament, and the first English Bible was soon to be printed. The Wycliffite text had no direct impact on the sixteenth-century versions or the King James Bible, but it certainly contributed to the spread of Bible literacy in England and to the creation of "a common pool of English Bible phrases."[5]

The text of the manuscript belonging to the Rare Bible Collection @ MOBIA is written in two columns with 35 lines to a full column. It is rubricated in red and blue and has ornamental initials, some of them in burnished gold. The American Bible Society acquired it from Bernard Quaritch in 1949. The opening shown here includes the beginning of the Gospel according to John.

2. New Testament

[Worms: Peter Schoeffer, 1526]
Facsimile edition, London: Paradine, 1976
8°: A-Z⁸ AA-BB⁸, Aa-Ss⁸ Tt⁴; 348 ff. 122 x 69 mm. Black letter. Herbert 2

The printing press was introduced in England in 1476, but was not used to produce Scriptures until the 1530s. The earliest English translations of the Bible were printed on the Continent. They were the work of William Tyndale (1494–1536), a priest and scholar who devoted his entire life to translating the Bible into English and earned a martyr's crown in the process. Born in Gloucestershire and educated at Oxford, Tyndale went to London in 1523 and tried to win for his translation the patronage of Bishop Cuthbert Tunstall. Rejected by Tunstall, Tyndale left England for Germany, probably in April 1524. One year later, while his translation of the New Testament was being printed in Cologne, the printer's shop was raided. Tyndale salvaged his manuscripts and at least some of the printed sheets and took refuge in Worms, where Peter Schoeffer issued in 1526 the first printed edition of the New Testament in English. In Cologne, Tyndale had been denounced as a Lutheran and through the last years of his life his enemies maintained that his English Bible was just the prelude to a Lutheran takeover of England.[6] Luther's influence on Tyndale's translation is undeniable. The 1525 Cologne fragment, which survives in one copy only, includes a Prologue modeled on Luther's Prologue to the September New Testament and some 90 marginal notes, most of which are taken from Luther's translation.

6. Daniell 2003: 143, 154; Pollard 1911: 117–118 (= 55–56 in the facsimile edition).

In his address *To the Reader* printed at the end of the 1526 New Testament, Tyndale pointed out that he had no English models for his translation. He obviously did not use the Wycliffite version and may not have been aware of its existence. He based his work on the Greek text while also consulting Erasmus' Latin translation of the New Testament, the Vulgate, and Luther's German version. Tyndale was striving for clarity and faithfulness to the original text. What he created was a uniquely beautiful translation that was copied and imitated in almost all later English versions of the Bible. Phrases we read in the King James Bible, such as *Ask and it shall be given you; seek and ye shall find; knock and it shall be opened unto you,* were first printed in Tyndale's New Testament. Scholars have tried to give a precise quantitative value to Tyndale's impact on the King James translation. Predictably, their results vary quite widely. For John Nielson and Royal Skousen writing in 1998, 83% of the King James Bible goes back to Tyndale; for Charles C. Butterworth writing in 1941 the figure is only 18 percent.[7] Quite apart from these academic exercises, Tyndale's influence on the 1611 translation can be recognized in each and every page of the New Testament, the Pentateuch, and the historical books.

7. Daniell 2003: 151–152 and 805 n. 13

The aborted edition of 1525 was to be printed in 3,000 copies and the 1526 edition may have had the same press run. Copies of the complete New Testament reached London before October 23, 1526, when Bishop Tunstall declared it a

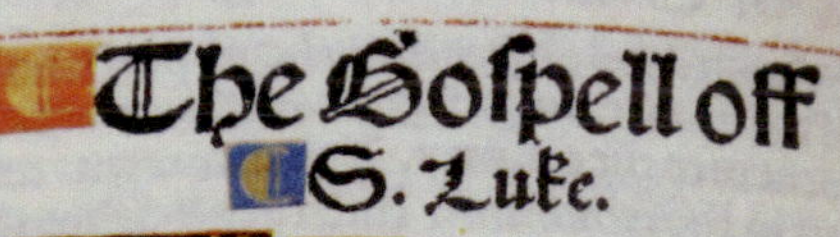# The Gospell off S. Luke.

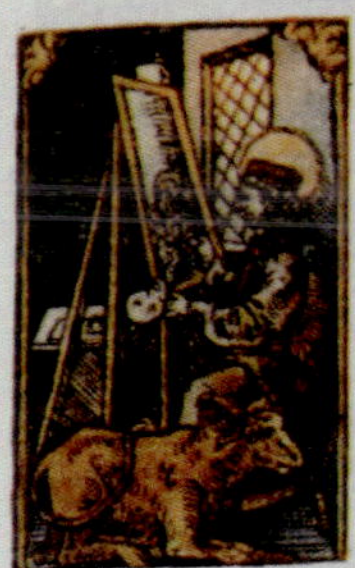Or as moche as ma/
ny have taken in hond to
compyle a treates off thoo thyn/
gs / which are surely knowen as
monge vs / even as they decla/
red them vnto vs / which from
the begynnynge sawe them with
their eyes / and were misters at
the doyng: I determined also /
as sone as I had searched out di
ligently all thing from the begynnynge / that the
I wolde wryte vnto the / goode Theophilus / th
at thou myghtest knowe the certente off thoo thi
gs / whereof thou arte informed.

The Fyrst. Chapter.

In the tyme of Herode kynge of iewry / there
was a certayne prest named Zacarias / off
the course of Abie. And his wyfe was of the do/
ughters of Aaron: And her name was Elizabe/
th. Booth were perfect before god / and walked
in all the lawes ād ordinacions of the lorde that
no mā coulde fynde fawte with them. And they
had no childe / be cause that Elisabeth was bar/
ren / And booth were wele stricken in age.

Hit cam to passe / as he executed the prestes of/
fice / before god as his course cām (accordinge
to the custome of the prestes office) his lott was
to bren odours / And went into the tempte of the

forbidden book not to be read within his diocese. Any person owning the book was to surrender it within 30 days under pain of excommunication. Four days later, on October 27, the Bishop presided over a ceremonial burning of Tyndale's New Testament in front of St. Paul's Cathedral. More copies were burned over the next few years and many people were tried for possessing or distributing them. The destruction of Tyndale's 1526 New Testament was so complete that only three copies are known to exist today.

Tyndale had earned Tunstall's enmity by being a Lutheran, by producing an English translation of the New Testament, and by basing it on the Greek text rather than the Latin Vulgate. Thomas More (1478–1535), who shared the Bishop's views and wrote lengthy polemical treatises against Tyndale, was particularly incensed by what he considered an unacceptable rendering of ecclesiastical terms in the 1526 New Testament. He strongly objected to the use of words such as *seniors, congregation, love,* and *repent* instead of the traditional *priest, church, charity* and *do penance.* Tyndale, who in 1536 would face death without recanting, did not dismiss More's criticism without carefully considering it. Some of the changes he introduced in the 1534 revision of the New Testament are based on More's remarks. He replaced the antiquated *seniors,* although not with *priests,* as More wanted, but with *elders.* He also adopted More's translation of the opening words in John's Gospel and printed the unforgettable line: *In the beginning was the word, and the word was with God, and the word was God.*[8] This verse found its way into the King James Bible, as did many verses and phrases originating in Tyndale's 1534 New Testament.

Tyndale's translation of the New Testament, though rejected by ecclesiastical and civil authorities, was avidly read in England. For the first ten years it was reprinted only in Antwerp, sometimes without Tyndale's knowledge or consent. Few copies survive and several early editions are known only through references in contemporary documents. The earliest Tyndale New Testament in the Rare Bible Collection @ MOBIA dates from 1548. The facsimile shown here is open at the beginning of Luke's Gospel.

8. See also Norton 2000: 22, 25

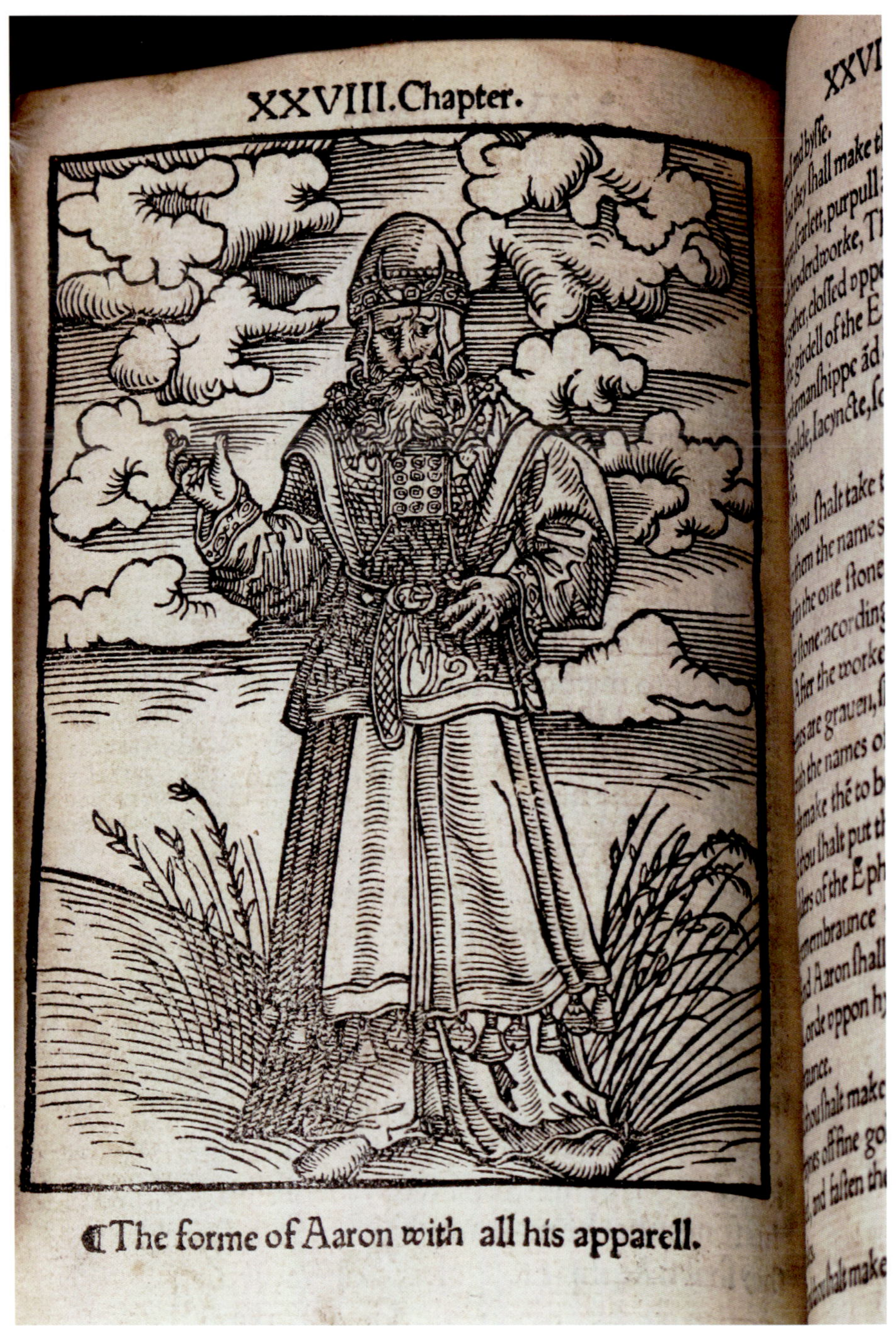

¶ The forme of Aaron with all his apparell.

3. Pentateuch

 | [ANTWERP: JOHANNES HOOCHSTRATEN], 1530

8°: [unsigned]⁸, B-L⁸; 88 ff.; [unsigned]⁸, A-I⁸ K⁴; 84 ff.; A⁸, A-F⁸ G⁴; 60 ff.; A¹⁰, B-I⁸ K⁴; 78 ff.; A⁴, B-I⁸; 68 ff. Total 378 ff. 128 x 65 mm. Black letter and roman type. Herbert 4

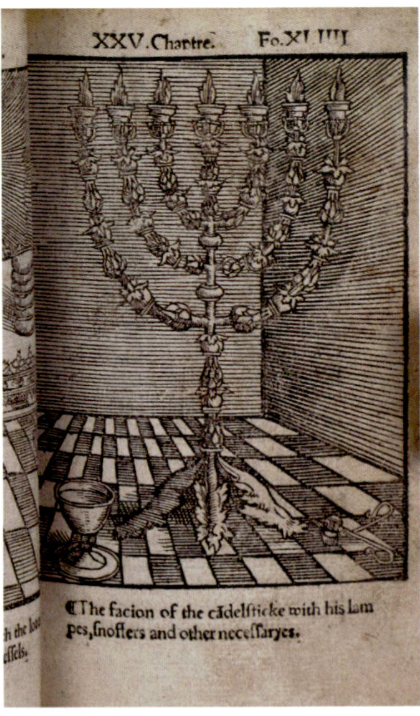

Fig. 3.1

The publication of the 1526 New Testament was followed on January 17, 1530 by an English translation of the Psalter done by George Joye and one day later by Tyndale's translation of the Pentateuch. A colophon placed at the end of Genesis indicates the exact date of its release while also attributing its printing to Hans Lufft in Marburg. There is proof that the book was printed in Antwerp by Johannes Hoochstraten. The false imprint must have been a kind of joke meant to disorient the authorities since Lufft, whose name can be translated as "thin air," was actually Luther's printer in Wittenberg.

Tyndale based his translation of the Pentateuch on the Hebrew text, just as he had based his New Testament on the original Greek. We can reasonably assume that he also used the available Latin versions, including the Vulgate and Sanctes Pagninus' 16th century work, and Luther's German translation of the Pentateuch first published in 1523. In an emotional statement at the end of his general prologue, Tyndale declares his willingness to accept corrections if the Hebrew text does not support his translation and mentions the very real possibility of his being "disallowed and also burnt." He also refers to the Hebrew text in the lists of unfamiliar words he appended to Genesis and Exodus and in his marginal notes.

Many of Tyndale's notes include attacks on the Pope and the Catholic doctrine, prelates, or priests. Of the 120 notes that contain more than one single word, 22 have disparaging remarks about the Pope, a dozen criticize the prelates and priests, and two mention "the popish" or "the papists." This is not what a modern reader would expect to find in a translation of the Bible, but verbal violence was not uncommon in the sixteenth century. A second edition of the Pentateuch including a slight revision of Genesis was issued in 1534 and reprinted in 1537. The three notes attacking the Pope in Genesis were dropped from these editions. Given time, Tyndale may have decided to remove all the offensive notes.

The five books of Tyndale's Pentateuch have separate foliation and were set in two distinct typefaces: Genesis and Numbers are printed in black letter, Exodus,

Leviticus, and Deuteronomy, in roman type. Exodus is illustrated with 11 full-page woodcuts similar to those used in a Dutch Bible printed in 1528, a Latin Bible printed in 1529, and Luther's Pentateuch of 1523.

The first edition of Tyndale's Pentateuch did not fare much better than his New Testament. Fewer than ten copies survive. The one that belongs in the Rare Bible Collection @ MOBIA is incomplete: it lacks everything before Genesis 50, the last folio of the word list in Genesis, the Prologue to Exodus, folios B2 and F8 in Exodus, and everything after the Prologue to Numbers. It is open to show Aaron in his priestly vestments (Exodus 28). A woodcut representing the seven-branched candelabrum (Exodus 25) is shown in Fig. 3.1.

Tyndale managed to print in 1531 his translation of Jonah, a biblical book Luther valued so much that he published it separately in 1526.[9] Only one copy survives, bound with other works in the British Library. The translator who had done so much for the English bible was not allowed to complete his work. Tyndale was arrested in May 1535, was tried and condemned as a heretic in August 1536, and suffered martyrdom early in October. He was mercifully strangled before being burned. His manuscript translation of the historical books of the Old Testament was later included in Matthew's Bible (see Cat. 5).

9. Daniell 1992: xxxvi

[MARBURG?: E. CERVICORNUS AND J. SOTER?], 1535

2°: †⁸, a-p⁶, 2a-2v⁶ 2A-2H⁶ 2I⁴, 3A-3R⁶, A-O⁶, 2A-2T⁶; 570 ff. 278 x 186 mm. Black letter. Herbert 18

This Bible is the first printed edition of the complete English text, its *editio princeps*. It was translated single-handedly by Miles Coverdale (1488–1568), who remains to this day the only British translator of the entire Bible into English. The colophon of Coverdale's Bible gives the exact date of its release: October 4, 1535, but fails to mention the printer(s) and place of publication. The title page does not mention them either. The book was certainly printed on the Continent, where Coverdale was living in exile since about 1528. Unfortunately, the translator's whereabouts are uncertain. He returned to Cambridge in 1531, but did not stay long in England. In 1534 he was working intently on his translation and was residing in the Low Countries or the Rhineland. L.A. Sheppard suggested in 1935 that Coverdale's Bible was printed by Eucharius Hirtzhorn or Cervicornus and Johann Heil or Soter in Marburg or maybe in Cologne. He argued that the woodblocks used to print the initials in the 1535 English Bible belonged to these two German printers.[10] More recently, Guido Lattré[11] asserted that the Bible was printed in Antwerp by Martin L'Empereur or Martin de Keyser, the printer who had produced the first French Bible in 1530. Coverdale was certainly associated with de Keyser's shop during the 1530s and received financial help from a citizen of Antwerp named Jacob van Meteren, but this does not necessarily prove Lattré's thesis.

Coverdale's knowledge of Greek and Hebrew was minimal and he freely admitted he had used five different translations in crafting his own version. The five translations have been identified as Tyndale's English New Testament and Pentateuch (Cats. 2 and 3), Luther's German version of the Bible printed between 1522 and 1534, the German version of Ulrich Zwingli and Leo Juda printed in Zurich between 1524 and 1529, the Latin Vulgate, and the Latin translation of Sanctes Pagninus dating from 1528. In the New Testament, Coverdale took Tyndale's version of 1534 as his base text, but revised it in the light of the two German versions.[12] The influence of the two Latin versions is most visible in the Old Testament.

In his dedication to Henry VIII, Coverdale made clear his intention to avoid sectarian controversies. In the area of ecclesiastical vocabulary he followed some of Tyndale's innovations and used *congregation, elders,* and *love* for *church, priests,* and *charity,* but he also alternated *repentance* with *penance* and *repent* with *do penance, amend, convert,* and even *turn.*[13] To help the reader he added short chapter summaries at the beginning of each section of the Bible and marginal notes that deal with cross-references and textual problems and do not have a polemical character.

The 1535 folio was printed in Schwabacher type, the standard typeface in contemporary German lands. It was embellished with ornamental initials and

10. Mozley 1953: 74–77

11. Lattré 2000: 90–99

12. Mozley 1953:86, 98

13. Mozley 1953:106

The first dayes worke.

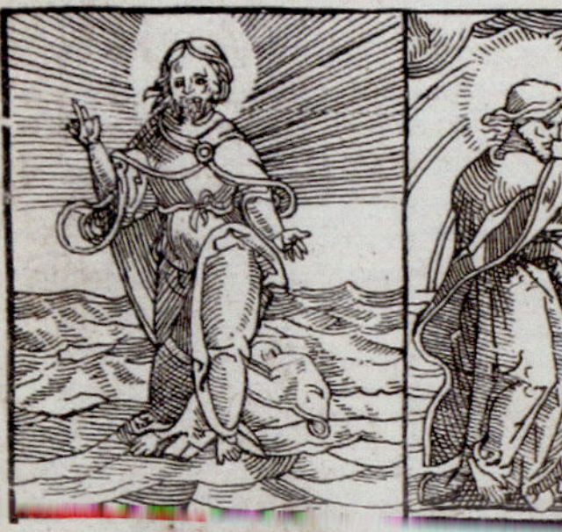

The seconde dayes worke.

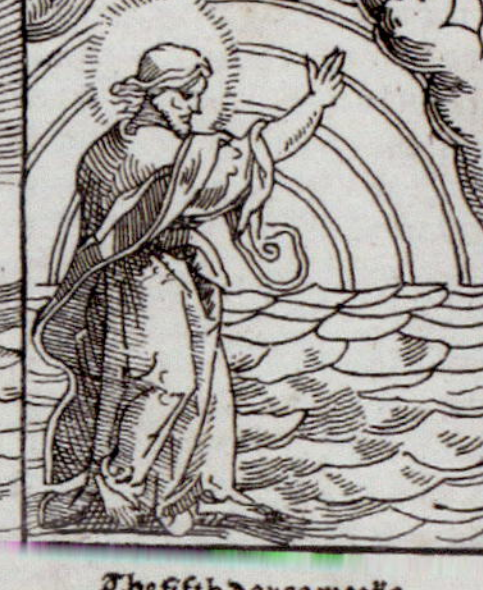

The thirde dayes worke.

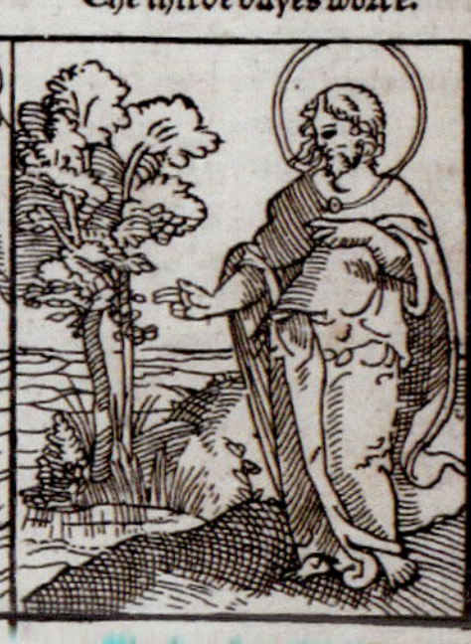

The fourth dayes worke.

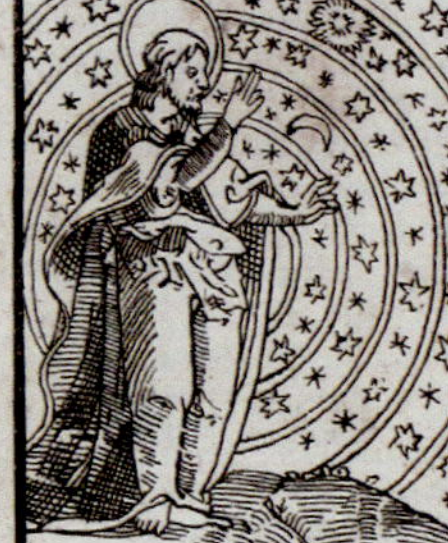

The fifth dayes worke.

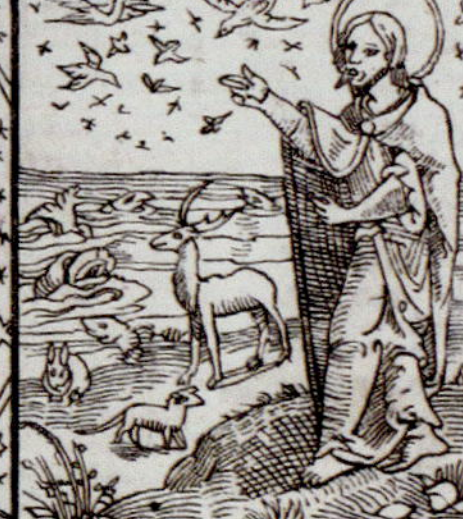

The sixte dayes worke.

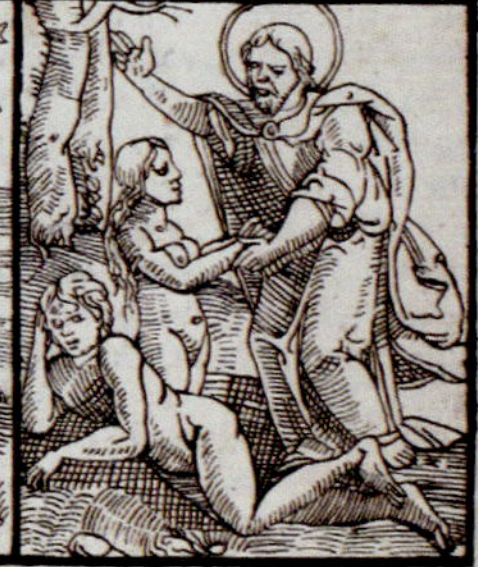

The first Chapter.

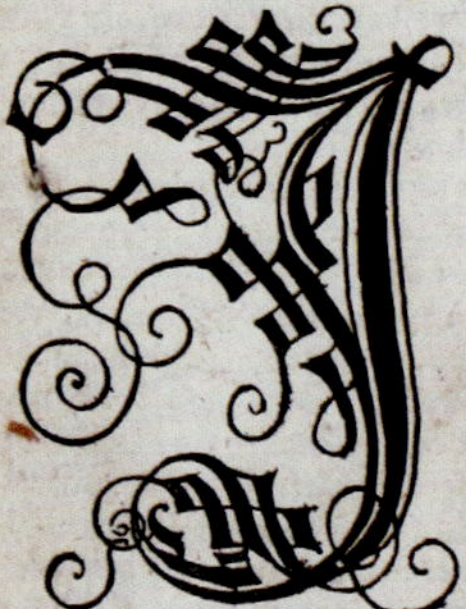

In ÿ begynnynge God created heauen ⁊ earth: and ÿ earth was voyde and emptie and darcknes was vpon the depe, ⁊ ÿ sprete of God moued vpõ the water. And God sayde: let there be light, ⁊ there was light. And God sawe the light that it was good. Then God deuyded ÿ light from the darcknes, and called the light, Daye: and the darcknes, Night. Then of the euenynge and mornynge was made the first daye.

And God sayde: let there be a firmament betwene the waters, and let it deuyde ÿ waters a sunder. Then God made ÿ firmamẽt, and parted the waters vnder the firmamẽt, from the waters aboue the firmament: And so it came to passe. And God called ÿ firmament, Heauen. Then of the euenynge ⁊ mornynge was made the seconde daye.

And God sayde: let the waters vnder heauen gather thẽ selues vnto one place, ÿ the drye londe maye appeare. And so it came to passe. And God called ÿ drye londe, Earth: and the gatheringe together of waters called he, ÿ See. And God sawe ÿ it was good.

And God sayde: let ÿ earth bringe forth grene grasse and herbe, that beareth sede: ⁊ frutefull trees, that maye beare frute, euery one after his kynde, hauynge their owne sede in them selues vpon the earth. And so it came to passe. And the earth brought forth grene grasse and herbe, ÿ beareth sede euery one after his kynde, ⁊ trees bearinge frute, ⁊

Iob 26.b
Pro 8.c

a

158 small woodcuts printed from 68 separate blocks, one of which was repeated 11 times. The title page, sadly missing from almost all surviving copies, is attributed to Holbein. The smaller woodcuts are crude copies of a set executed by Hans Sebald Beham (1500–1550) and used by Christian Egenolff to print a German Bible in 1534 in Frankfurt. Like most sixteenth-century Bibles, the Coverdale folio is more heavily illustrated in the Old Testament than in the New. Women are almost totally absent from its woodcuts. Only Eve and Bathsheba make a timid appearance.[14]

14. Daniell 2003: 186

Coverdale is at his best in the Psalter and the prophetical books of the Old Testament, which remain his most enduring legacy. Phrases familiar to all readers of the English Bible go back to his 1535 translation: *tender mercies* (Psalm 25:6), *loving kindness* (ibid.), *seek the Lord while he may be found* (Isaiah 55:6), and many others. They were included in the so-called Great Bible of 1539 (see Cat. 6) and were later incorporated into the King James Bible.

The Bible is open to show the beginning of Genesis with its woodcuts representing the six days of Creation and its beautiful initial.

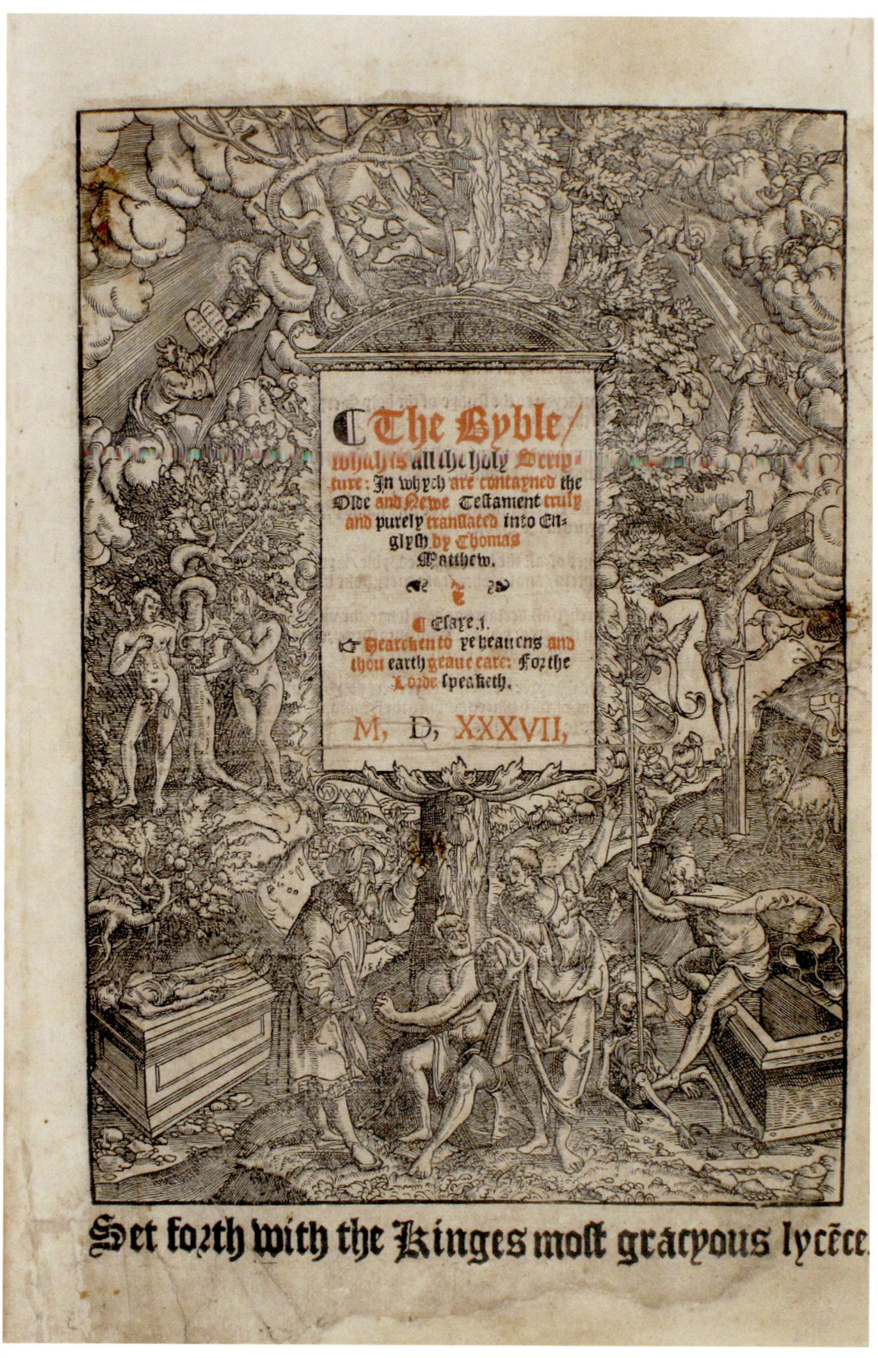

5. Bible with Apocrypha

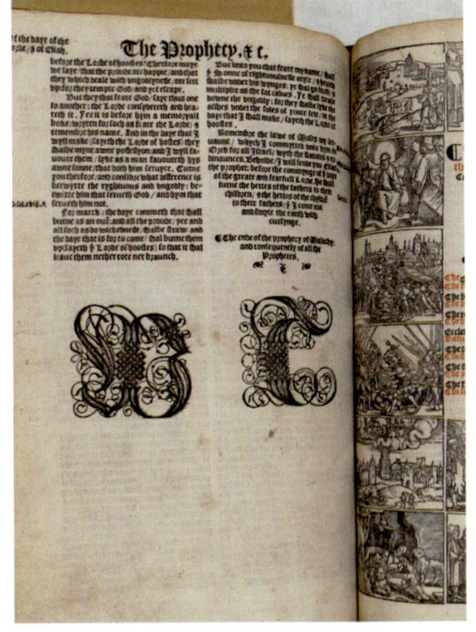

Fig. 5.1

15. Pollard 1911: 215 (= 94 in the facsimile edition)

On August 4, 1537 Thomas Cranmer (1489–1556), Archbishop of Canterbury, sent Thomas Cromwell (1485–1540), Lord Privy Seal, one copy of a recently printed English Bible he described as a new translation and a good one. Cranmer hoped the King would license the Bible to be freely sold and read in England. His fellow bishops had already agreed to work on their own translation of the Bible, but Cranmer believed they would not complete the task "till a day after doomsday."[15]

The title page of the new Bible, printed in red and black, deliberately concealed the true names of its translators and failed to mention the publishers and place of publication. The biblical text was not translated by the fictitious Thomas Matthew, as indicated in the printed title, but was put together by combining Tyndale's Pentateuch and New Testament with Coverdale's translation of the sections including Ezra to Malachi and the Apocrypha, and with a previously unpublished version of Joshua to 2 Chronicles. Tyndale had been executed for heresy ten months before the publication of the 1537 Bible and Coverdale was known as a Lutheran and was probably living in exile at the time. The person responsible for putting together the 1537 Bible prudently decided to replace their names with a *nom de plume* that evoked two of the Apostles.

That person was John Rogers (*c.* 1500–1555), a scholar educated in Cambridge and Wittenberg, Tyndale's friend and coworker, a pastor who was to become the first victim of the persecution launched by Queen Mary against the Protestants.[16] In addition to combining the various sections of the translation, Rogers also provided all the notes and additional texts in the 1537 Bible. He was a proficient linguist and his more than 2,100 notes prove that he had studied the Hebrew text, the Aramaic Targums, the Septuagint, and various Patristic commentaries to the Bible, as well as several German and Dutch translations and the French versions of Lefèvre d'Etaples and Olivétan. He was certainly qualified to translate the historical books of the Old Testament, from Joshua to 2 Chronicles, but compelling stylistic evidence indicates that these books were translated by William Tyndale. External evidence confirms this view: Halle's

16. Mozley 1953: 136–40

Chronicle of 1548 ascribes these books to Tyndale and Foxe maintains that John Rogers translated only one book: the Prayer of Manasseh.[17] We must assume that Rogers had access to a manuscript copy of Tyndale's translation the Procurer-General Pierre Dufief failed to discover in May 1535, when he searched Tyndale's lodgings in Antwerp and confiscated his property.

Matthew's Bible was printed in Antwerp, probably by Matthew Crom, for the London printers Richard Grafton (*c.* 1513–1573) and Edward Whitchurch (d. 1561), who financed its publication to the tune of 500 pounds. The press run was 1,500 copies. Henry VIII granted the publishers' request and allowed them to print on the title page the words: *Set forth with the King's gracious license.* Henry VIII also issued a proclamation to his justices requesting that each shire should have a copy of the Bible. Several Bishops gave similar orders to the parishes in their dioceses.[18]

The 1537 Bible is beautifully illustrated with woodcuts similar to those used in Luther's December 1522 New Testament and in a Low German Bible printed in Lubeck in 1533. At the end of the prefatory material two sets of ornamental initials stand for John Rogers and Henricus Rex. The publishers' initials, R G and E C, are found before the Prophets and William Tyndale's initials are printed at the end of the Old Testament, before the Apocrypha (Fig. 5.1).

Matthew's Bible was short-lived, but its influence on future English translations was durable. It ensured the survival of Tyndale's translation of the Old Testament and made possible the publication of the Great Bible in 1539 (see Cat. 6), which ultimately led to the King James translation of 1611.

17. Mozley 1953: 150–153, Daniell 1992: xxv–xxvi

18. Pollard 1911: 220 (= 96 in the facsimile edition), Mozley 1953: 167–179

[LONDON]: RICHARD GRAFTON AND EDWARD WHITCHURCH, 1539

2°: ⋆⁶, a-k⁸ I⁴, A-P⁸ Q⁴, 2A-2P⁸ 2Q-2R⁶, 3A-3K⁸, 2A-2N⁸; 530 ff. 337 x 235 mm. Black letter. Herbert 46

The two influential sponsors of Matthew's Bible, Thomas Cranmer and Thomas
Cromwell, knew that its press run of 1,500 copies was hardly adequate for a kingdom comprising some 9,000 parishes. They also understood that conservative
bishops, such as Gardiner or Tunstall, would never accept a Bible including
Tyndale's Prologue to Romans and John Roger's marginal notes. Their decision
to promote a revision of the recently published Bible appears as almost inevitable.
The task of revising Matthew's Bible was entrusted to Miles Coverdale, who
did not try to push forward his own translation, but selflessly strived to make
Tyndale's version acceptable in Henry VIII's England. He had less than one year
to complete the work, for the 1537 Bible arrived in London in August 1537 and the
printing of its revised form began in Paris in May 1538.

Coverdale went to Paris to help Richard Grafton and Edward Whitchurch
print the revised Bible. Grafton and Whitchurch had already printed Matthew's
Bible in Antwerp and had arranged with the French printer François Regnault
to use his shop for producing the new edition. Cromwell had chosen Paris as the
right place to print the Bible because he believed that good quality paper and
skilled workers were available only there. The printers' work progressed rapidly
for a few months, but came to a stop when the Inquisition raided Regnault's shop.
The English proofreaders fled, Regnault was arrested, and the printed sheets were
confiscated. Some sheets were burned in Paris, some were sent back to England
after protracted negotiations. The details and ramifications of the incident are not
entirely clear. An edition of 3,000 copies was released in London in April 1539 and

19. Daniell 2003: 200–203   came to be known as "the Great Bible."[19] Cromwell had requested that a copy of
this Bible be displayed in every parish by Christmas 1538 and surviving records
show that many parishes purchased both a Bible and a chain to fasten it to pews,
pulpits or columns. The overall demand for Bibles determined the publishers to
issue six additional editions between April 1540 and December 1541. The second
edition, released in April 1540, includes a beautiful preface written by Archbishop
Thomas Cranmer and bears on its title page an inscription that indicates its status:
This is the Bible appointed to the use of the churches.

Coverdale had no direct access to the original Hebrew and Greek texts and
used Latin translations in revising Matthew's Bible. He checked the New Testament
against Erasmus' Latin version and aimed for consistency and exactitude. In
the Old Testament he based his revision on Sebastian Münster's Latin translation

20. Mozley 1953: 221–238   first published in Basel in 1535.[20] For the April 1539 edition, Coverdale revised
thoroughly the sections of Matthew's Bible that had been translated by Tyndale
(Genesis to Ezra and the New Testament), but left untouched the sections taken
from his own translation (Esther to Malachi and the Apocrypha). In 1540 he made

The Psalmes of Dauid,

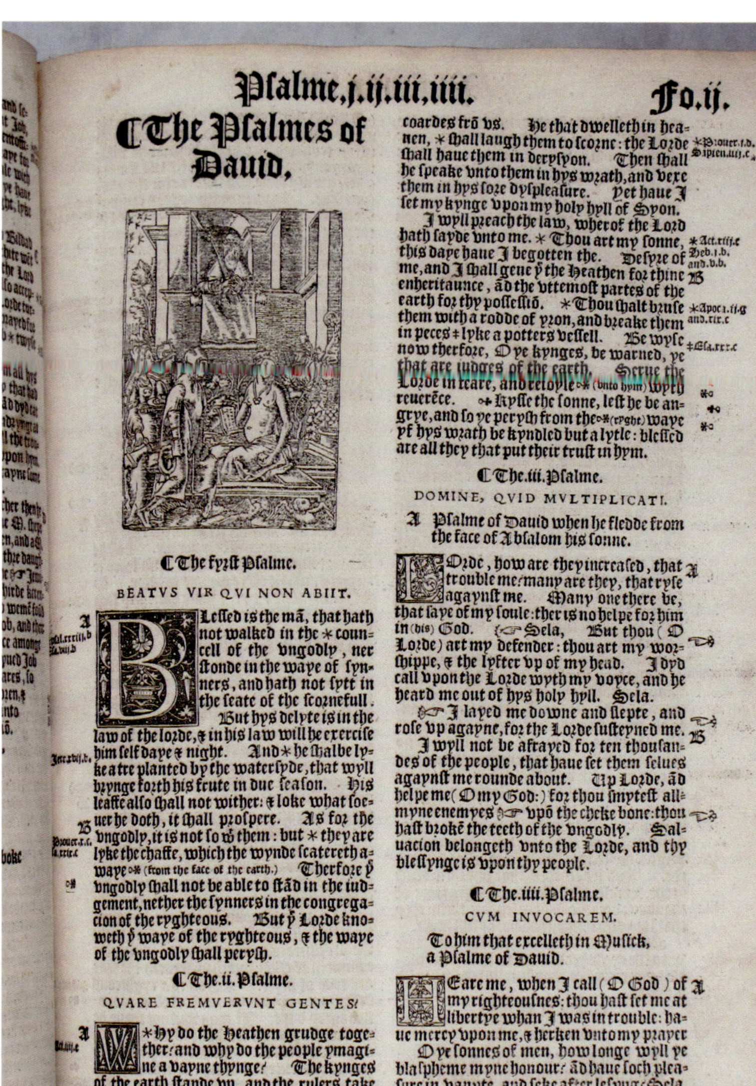

The fyrst Psalme.

BEATVS VIR QVI NON ABIIT.

Blessed is the man, that hath not walked in the *councell of the vngodly, ner stonde in the waye of synners, and hath not sytt in the seate of the scornefull. But hys delyte is in the law of the lorde, & in his law will he exercise him self daye & night. And *he shalbe lyke a tre planted by the water syde, that wyll brynge forth his frute in due season. His leaffe also shall not wither: & loke what soeuer he doth, it shall prospere. As for the vngodly, it is not so wt them: but *they are lyke the chaffe, which the wynde scatereth awaye *(from the face of the earth.) Therfore ye vngodly shall not be able to stad in the iudgement, nether the synners in the congregacion of the ryghteous. But ye Lorde knoweth ye waye of the ryghteous, & the waye of the vngodly shall perysh.

The. ij. Psalme.

QVARE FREMVERVNT GENTES?

Why do the heathen grudge together: and why do the people ymagine a vayne thynge? The kynges of the earth stande vp, and the rulers take councell together *agaynst the Lorde, and agaynst hys anoynted. Let vs breake their bondes asunder, and cast awaye their coardes fro vs. He that dwelleth in heanen, *shall laugh them to scorne: the Lorde shall haue them in derysyon. Then shall he speake vnto them in hys wrath, and vexe them in hys sore dyspleasure. Yet haue I set my kynge vpon my holy hyll of Syon.

I wyll preach the law, wherof the Lord hath sayde vnto me. *Thou art my sonne, this daye haue I begotten the. Desyre of me, and I shall geue ye the Heathen for thine enheritaunce, ad the vttemost partes of the earth for thy possessio. *Thou shalt bruse them with a rodde of yron, and breake them in peces & lyke a potters vessell. Be wyse now therfore, O ye kynges, be warned, ye that are iudges of the earth, Serue the Lorde in feare, and reioyse *(vnto him) wyth reuerece. *Kysse the sonne, lest he be angrye, and so ye perysh from the *(ryght) waye yf hys wrath be kyndled but a lytle: blessed are all they that put their trust in hym.

The. iii. Psalme.

DOMINE, QVID MVLTIPLICATI.

A Psalme of Dauid when he fledde from the face of Absalom his sonne.

LOrde, how are they increased, that trouble me: many are they, that ryse agaynst me. Many one there be, that saye of my soule: ther is no helpe for him in (his) God. *Sela. But thou (O Lorde) art my defender: thou art my worshippe, & the lyfter vp of my head. I dyd call vpon the Lorde wyth my voyce, and he heard me out of hys holy hyll. Sela.

* I layed me downe and slepte, and rose vp agayne, for the Lorde susteyned me. I wyll not be afrayed for ten thousandes of the people, that haue set them selues agaynst me rounde about. Up Lorde, ad helpe me (O my God:) for thou smytest all myne enemyes *vpo the cheke bone: thou hast broke the teeth of the vngodly. Saluacion belongeth vnto the Lorde, and thy blessynge is vpon thy people.

The. iiii. Psalme.

CVM INVOCAREM.

To him that excelleth in Musick, a Psalme of Dauid.

HEare me, when I call (O God) of my rightuousnes: thou hast set me at libertye whan I was in trouble: haue mercy vpon me, & herken vnto my prayer

O ye sonnes of men, how longe wyll ye blaspheme myne honour? ad haue soch pleasure in vanyte, and seke after lesyng? Sela.

Knowe thys also, that the Lorde hath chosen to hym selfe the man that is godly: when I call vpon the Lorde, he wyll heare me.

6 . Bible with Apocrypha

corrections to the book of Isaiah, but on the whole he did not alter significantly his 1535 text. The slightly revised form of the 1540 Psalter was included in the *Book of Common Prayer* of 1549 and continued to be used in the liturgy of the Anglican and Episcopalian churches until the 1960s.

Coverdale made several concessions to the conservative bishops. In places where the Vulgate paraphrases the original Greek or Hebrew texts, he printed the Vulgate additions in smaller type and within brackets. He also removed the prefatory material and notes that had offended die-hard clergymen in Matthew's Bible: Olivétan's *Table of Principal Matters,* Tyndale's Prologue to Romans, and many marginal notes.

The 1539 Bible includes several woodcuts and a striking title page that is unfortunately lacking from most surviving copies. The title identifies it in red letters as "the Bible in English" while all the biblical texts scattered over the page are given in Latin. In the upper register, Henry is enthroned under a small representation of God with the Archbishop of Canterbury, Thomas Cranmer, to his right and his "Vice Regent in Spirituals," Thomas Cromwell, to his left. Both stand bare-headed. In the middle register, the same Cranmer and Cromwell bearing appropriate head gear and identified by their shields distribute Bibles titled *Verbum Dei,* while in the lower register a large multitude acclaims *Vivat Rex* and two figures that may represent children utter the only English texts in the woodcut: *God Save the King.* Below the Archbishop, a preacher gives a sermon on 1 Timothy 2 and below the Vice Regent looms the ominous depiction of Newgate Prison.[21] The opening page of the Book of Psalms includes a small woodcut representing David and Bathsheba, a large initial at the beginning of Psalm 1 and smaller initials at the beginning of Psalms 2–4.

As the first "authorized" English Bible, the text edited by Coverdale has an official character and a sober diction that would be transmitted to the King James Bible. There is a bitter irony in the fact that it introduced Tyndale's translation in every parish of Henry VIII's kingdom 13 years after the translator's death. Violent death or exile was to be the fate of the persons closely associated with the Great Bible. Thomas Cromwell was executed without trial on July 28, 1540. His shield was erased from all later editions of the Bible. Thomas Cranmer died at the stake under the reign of Queen Mary, on March 21, 1556. Miles Coverdale went into exile in 1540, returned in 1548, was Bishop of Exeter between 1551 and 1553, endured a third exile between 1553 and 1559, and died of old age in London on January 20, 1569.

21. Daniell 2003: 205–208

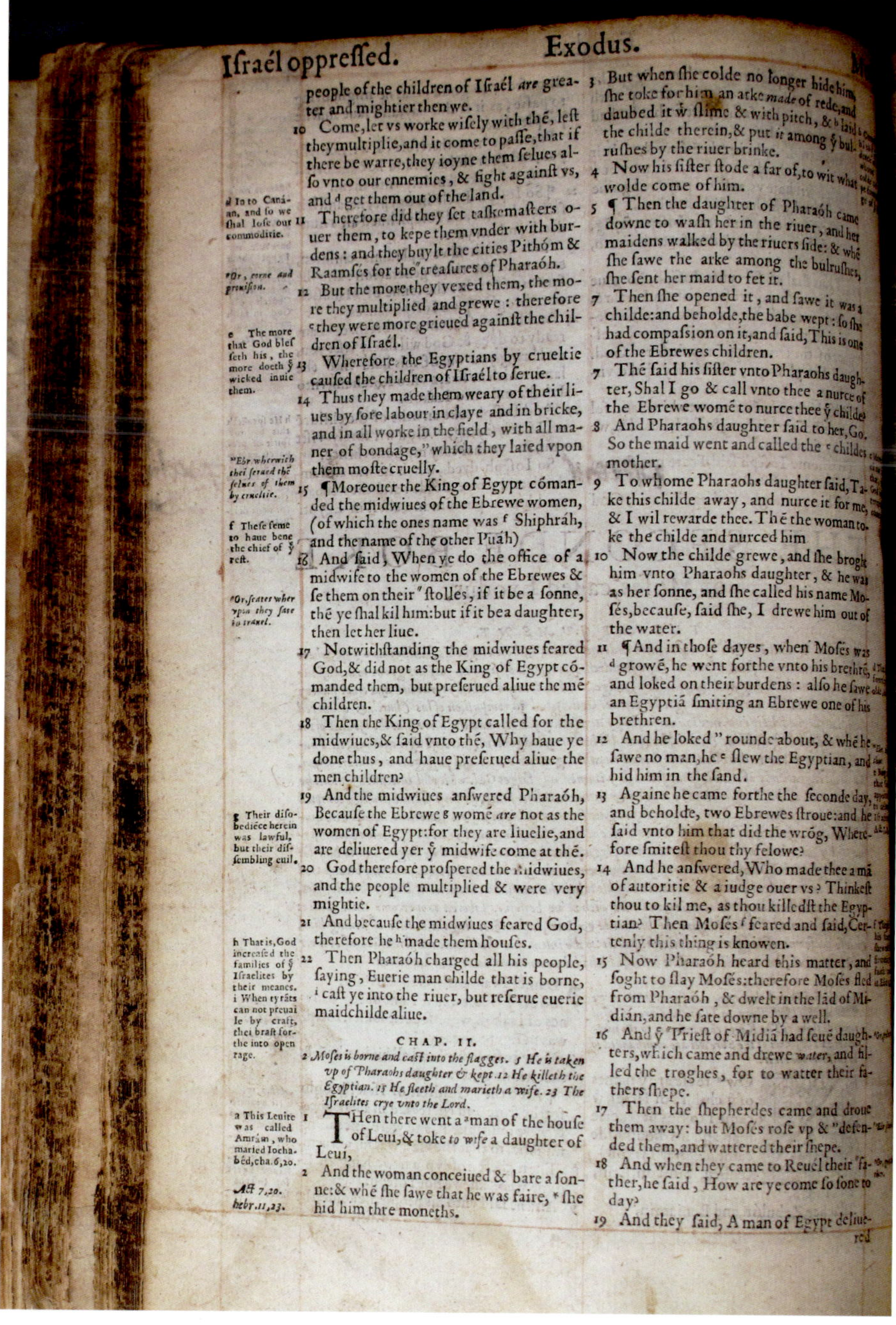

d In to Canáan, and so we shal lose our commoditie.

*Or, corne and prouision.

e The more that God blesseth his, the more doeth ÿ wicked inuie them.

"Ebr. wherwith thei serued thé selues of them by crueltie.

f These seme to haue bene the chief of ÿ rest.

*Or, seates wher ypon they sate to trauel.

g Their disobediéce herein was lawful, but their dissembling euil.

h That is, God increased the families of ÿ Israelites by their meanes.
i When tyráts can not preuaile by craft, thei brast forthe into open rage.

a This Leuite was called Amrám, who maried Iochabéd, cha.6,20.

Act 7,20. hebr.11,23.

people of the children of Israél *are* greater and mightier then we.

10 Come, let vs worke wisely with thé, lest they multiplie, and it come to passe, that if there be warre, they ioyne them selues also vnto our ennemies, & fight against vs, and d get them out of the land.

11 Therefore did they set taskemasters ouer them, to kepe them vnder with burdens: and they buylt the cities Pithóm & Raamsés for the "treasures of Pharaóh.

12 But the more they vexed them, the more they multiplied and grewe: therefore e they were more grieued against the children of Israél.

13 Wherefore the Egyptians by crueltie caused the children of Israél to serue.

14 Thus they made them weary of their liues by sore labour in claye and in bricke, and in all worke in the field, with all maner of bondage, "which they laied vpon them moste cruelly.

15 ¶ Moreouer the King of Egypt cómanded the midwiues of the Ebrewe women, (of which the ones name was f Shiphráh, and the name of the other Puáh)

16 And said, When ye do the office of a midwife to the women of the Ebrewes & se them on their "stolles, if it be a sonne, thé ye shal kil him: but if it be a daughter, then let her liue.

17 Notwithstanding the midwiues feared God, & did not as the King of Egypt cómanded them, but preserued aliue the mé children.

18 Then the King of Egypt called for the midwiues, & said vnto thé, Why haue ye done thus, and haue preserued aliue the men children?

19 And the midwiues answered Pharaóh, Because the Ebrewe s womé *are* not as the women of Egypt: for they are liuelie, and are deliuered yer ÿ midwife come at thé.

20 God therefore prospered the midwiues, and the people multiplied & were very mightie.

21 And because the midwiues feared God, therefore he h made them houses.

22 Then Pharaóh charged all his people, saying, Euerie man childe that is borne, i cast ye into the riuer, but reserue euerie maidchilde aliue.

CHAP. II.

2 Moses is borne and cast into the flagges. 5 He is taken up of Pharaohs daughter & kept. 12 He killeth the Egyptian. 15 He fleeth and marieth a wife. 23 The Israelites crye vnto the Lord.

1 THen there went a a man of the house of Leui, & toke *to wife* a daughter of Leui,

2 And the woman conceiued & bare a sonne: & whé she sawe that he was faire, * she hid him thre moneths.

3 But when she colde no longer hide him, she toke for him an arke *made* of rede, and daubed it wt slime & with pitch, & b laid the childe therein, & put *it* among ÿ bulrushes by the riuer brinke.

4 Now his sister stode a far of, to wit what wolde come of him.

5 ¶ Then the daughter of Pharaóh came downe to wash her in the riuer, and her maidens walked by the riuers side: & whé she sawe the arke among the bulrushes, she sent her maid to fet it.

6 Then she opened it, and sawe it was a childe: and beholde, the babe wept: so she had compassion on it, and said, This is one of the Ebrewes children.

7 Thé said his sister vnto Pharaohs daughter, Shal I go & call vnto thee a nurce of the Ebrewe womé to nurce thee ÿ childe?

8 And Pharaohs daughter said to her, Go. So the maid went and called the c childes mother.

9 To whome Pharaohs daughter said, Take this childe away, and nurce it for me, & I wil rewarde thee. Thé the woman toke the childe and nurced him.

10 Now the childe grewe, and she broght him vnto Pharaohs daughter, & he was as her sonne, and she called his name Moses, because, said she, I drewe him out of the water.

11 ¶ And in those dayes, when Moses was d growé, he went forthe vnto his brethré, and loked on their burdens: also he sawe an Egyptiá smiting an Ebrewe one of his brethren.

12 And he loked "rounde about, & whé he sawe no man, he e slew the Egyptian, and hid him in the sand.

13 Againe he came forthe the seconde day, and beholde, two Ebrewes stroue: and he said vnto him that did the wróg, Wherefore smitest thou thy felowe?

14 And he answered, Who made thee a má of autoritie & a iudge ouer vs? Thinkest thou to kil me, as thou killedst the Egyptian? Then Moses f feared and said, Certenly this thing is knowen.

15 Now Pharaóh heard this matter, and soght to slay Moses: therefore Moses fled from Pharaóh, & dwelt in the lád of Midián, and he sate downe by a well.

16 And ÿ Priest of Midiá had seué daughters, which came and drewe *water*, and filled the troghes, for to watter their fathers shepe.

17 Then the shepherdes came and droue them away: but Moses rose vp & "defended them, and wattered their shepe.

18 And when they came to Reuél their father, he said, How are ye come so sone to day?

19 And they said, A man of Egypt deliuered

GENEVA: ROWLAND HALL, 1560

4°: ★*★⁴, a-z⁴ A-2Z⁴ &⁶ 3A-5B⁴, 2A-3L⁴; 614 ff.; 218 x 139 mm. Herbert 107

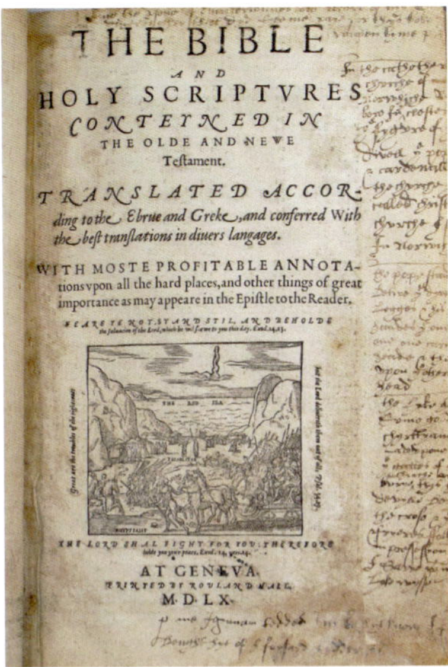

Fig. 7.1

After the accession of Queen Mary in July 1553, many Protestant ministers and scholars left her realm to seek refuge on the Continent. In October 1554 a group of Marian exiles including John Knox, the Scottish Reformer, William Whittingham, Anthony Gilby (*c.* 1510–1585), and Christopher Goodman (1520–1603) settled in Geneva and joined the circle of Calvin and Théodore de Bèze (better known as Beza, 1519–1605). They found an assembly of learned men with a passion for the Bible and a commitment to making it available to everyone. The Academy of Geneva was about to be inaugurated and the city's printers were busy setting the biblical text in Greek, Latin, Hebrew, French and Italian. A French version of the Bible prepared by Robert Olivétan, Calvin's cousin, had been available since 1535 and was revised in Geneva under Calvin's supervision in 1553. In the 1550s alone, this French translation was reprinted in Geneva by 15 different printers who produced some 30 editions of the complete Bible and about 26 editions of the New Testament.[22]

Inspired by the example of their French-speaking friends, the Marian exiles started planning their own English translation of the Bible, based on the original languages and provided with a running commentary that transformed it into a precursor of the modern Study Bibles. The New Testament was first published as a small octavo in June 1557 and was the work of William Whittingham (*c.* 1524–1579), an Oxford educated scholar who would be made Dean of Durham in 1563, under Queen Elizabeth. The text was essentially a revision Tyndale's translation as printed in 1548 by Richard Jugge with a few readings borrowed from the Great Bible that had been edited by Coverdale in 1539. The influence of Beza's Latin translation of 1556 is clearly visible throughout the whole volume.

Work on the Old Testament must have started soon after the publication of the 1557 New Testament, and kept the translators busy "for the space of two years and more, day and night."[23] It was complemented by a thorough revision of the New Testament, done probably by Whittingham. The team proudly acknowledged they had used the original Hebrew and Greek texts and compared

22. Chambers 1983: 167–263

23. *To the Reader,* [p. 1]. This document is dated 10 April 1560

them with a variety of vernacular translations. At the time, an English version of the Old Testament based on the Hebrew text existed only for the section including Genesis to 2 Chronicles and had been prepared by William Tyndale. The Pentateuch had been first published in 1530, while the historical books, from Joshua to 2 Chronicles became available through Matthew's Bible of 1537 and were revised in the Great Bible of 1539 (see Cat. 5 and 6). The second part of the Old Testament, from Ezra to Malachi, was first translated into English from Hebrew by Gilby and Goodman, the only members of the Geneva team who specialized in Hebrew. They were also responsible for the textual notes based on Rabbi David Kimhi's (1160–1235) commentary, most of which found their way into the King James Bible.

As emphasized in the translators' preface, the Geneva Bible had many features designed to facilitate the readers' access to the sacred text: book and chapter summaries, running titles indicating the content of each page, marginal notes, woodcuts, maps, and tables. Most of the notes explained "the hard places" in the Bible and were acceptable to readers belonging to all Christian denominations. A few of them, however, included controversial statements based on Calvin's theology. Already visible in the 1560 edition, the Calvinist orientation of the Geneva Bible became more explicit in the revised New Testament prepared by Lawrence Tomson (1539–1608) in 1576 and attained its most virulent form in the notes to Revelation originally written in Latin by Franciscus Junius (1545–1602), and first printed in English in 1592.

In its 1560 form, the Geneva Bible was readily accepted by both the general public and the English clergy. It was frequently used by contemporary preachers, was quoted by Shakespeare and Milton and was brought to America by the Pilgrims. Prior to the publication of the King James Bible in 1611, the Geneva version was the most frequently reprinted English translation. According to Herbert's catalogue, the standard bibliography for English Bibles published up to 1961, by the early 1630s there had been 120 editions of the Geneva text, 49 of the Bishops' Bible, 32 of the Great Bible, and 27 of Coverdale's version. Most editions of the Geneva text were produced in small and popular sizes, as quartos and octavos.

The Geneva Bible competed successfully against the 1568 Bishops' Bible that was actively promoted by the established Church of England. Its demise was linked to the publication of the King James text. The Bible of the Marian exiles ceased to be printed in London after 1616, though it was sporadically reprinted in Amsterdam until the end of the century.

As reported by William Barlow in his account of the Hampton Court Conference discussed in the following section,[24] James was extremely hostile to

24. Barlow 1604: 46–47, see Cat. 11

the Geneva Bible. He complained about the antimonarchical character of the Geneva notes to Exodus 1:19 and 2 Chronicles 15:16. In Exodus, the decision of the Hebrew midwives to spare the male infants and disobey Pharaoh's command is considered "lawful, but their dissembling evil" while in 2 Chronicles King Asa is condemned for failing to kill his mother as punishment for her idolatry. James apparently read this note as an exhortation to regicide. He may also have been painfully reminded of the execution of his own mother, Mary Queen of Scots. On the other hand, the Geneva translators probably expressed their feelings for Queen Mary, their persecutor, by repeatedly using the word "tyrant" in their notes and their biblical text.[25]

The five maps and 26 woodcuts included in the 1560 edition enable the reader to visualize biblical events and objects. These illustrations are found only in the Pentateuch, 1–2 Kings, and Ezekiel. Many of them are borrowed from contemporary French Bibles and have retained French phrases such as *Midi, Orient, Le Parvis de dedans* ("South, East, the Inner Court").

The influence of the Greek, Latin, and French Geneva Bibles is visible in the graphic design of the English version. Like its models, the 1560 English Bible is printed in roman type and has the verse division that originated in the Greek New Testament published by Robert Estienne in 1551 and was extended to the complete Bible in the French version of 1553 and the Latin edition of 1555. In England, the Bishops' Bible adopted the division into verses in 1568 and the King James in 1611. The black letter type continued to be used until the 1650s; it had been used occasionally to print the Geneva version since 1578.

The translators of the King James Bible were wise enough to disregard their sovereign's dislike for the Geneva Bible and tacitly incorporated into their work many phrases taken from this excellent translation. They are indebted to the Geneva version for some of the best known verses in their own Bible, including the opening lines of Psalm 23: *The Lord is my shepherd, I shall not want*, etc.

The Bible is open to show the translators' note to Exodus 1:19. A photograph of its title page is printed as Fig. 7.1.

25. See Gn 4:1, Argument to Joshua, Argument to 1 Samuel; Job 6:23, 15:20, 27:13, Ps 54:3 etc. The word *tyrant* does not appear in the King James Bible; *mighty* and *oppressor* are used in the verses quoted above.

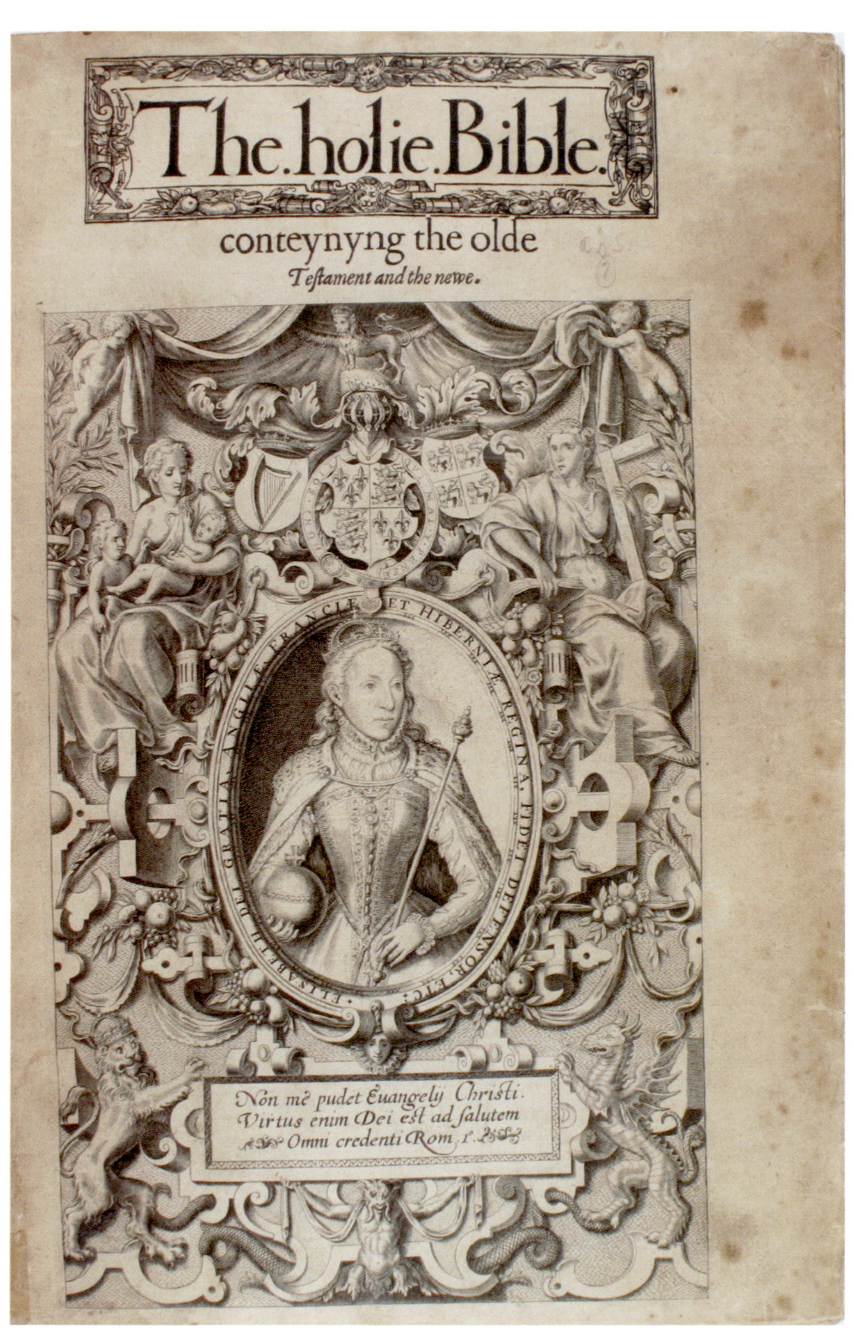

8 . Bible with Apocrypha

8. Bible with Apocrypha

LONDON: RICHARD JUGGE, 1568

2°: πj⁸ ✶¹⁰ ✶⁸?, A-Q⁸, A-Y⁸ Z¹⁰, A-E⁸ F⁶ G-Z⁸ 2A⁸ 2B¹², A-O⁸ P⁶, A-V⁸; 818 ff. (?); 356 x 238 mm.
Black letter. Herbert 125

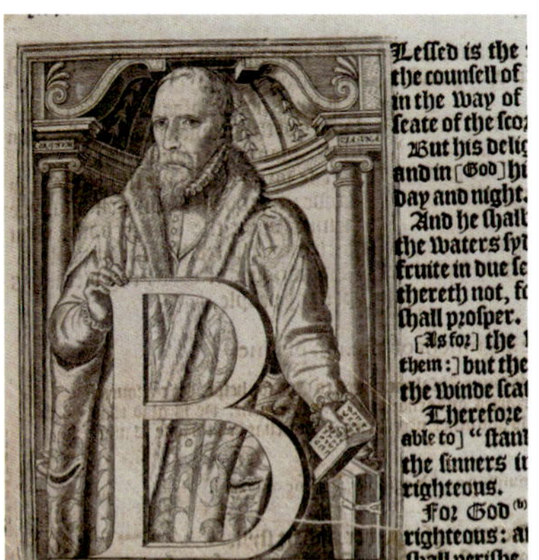

Fig. 8.1

The last Catholic Archbishop of Canterbury, Reginald Pole, died a few hours after Queen Mary, on November 17, 1558, and was succeeded by Elizabeth's nominee, Matthew Parker, in December 1559. Under the new queen, owning or reading the Bible in English ceased to be a capital crime and the Geneva version spread rapidly throughout the kingdom. Archbishop Parker (1504–1575) made no efforts to suppress the Puritan translation, but prevented it from being printed in England. Like many members of the Anglican clergy, he did not consider it appropriate for liturgical use. Since 1539, the English version endorsed by the established Church had been the Great Bible revised by Coverdale (see Cat. 6). Matthew Parker decided it was time to correct and update this version. The idea may have originated with Richard Cox (*c.* 1500–1581), the Bishop of Ely, who mentioned it in January 1561, in a letter addressed to William Cecil, Queen Elizabeth's chief advisor. By November 1566, Archbishop Parker reported to Cecil that the work was well under way. By September 1568 the Bible had already been printed and Cecil was asked to offer the Queen a specially bound presentation copy.[26]

26. See Pollard 1911: 291–295 (= 122–124 in the facsimile edition)

Such speed of execution was achieved by distributing the work among many scholars. To stimulate their interest in the project, Parker decided to give due credit to each contributor and actually included their initials, if not their full names, in the printed edition. Only a small group of insiders could decode the system, but it was nevertheless an unprecedented form of recognition. In some cases the initials were printed inside the first ornamental capital letter of a book, in others they were recorded the end of a book or group of books. Parker's initials, *MC* for *Matthaeus Cantuariensis* "Matthew of Canterbury," are found at the beginning of most of the books he revised: Genesis and Exodus, Matthew and Mark, 2 Corinthians-Hebrews. The initials *RE* at the end of Luke and John refer to Richard Cox, the Bishop of Ely. The list of contributors also includes Edmund Grindal (*c.* 1519–1583), Edwin Sandys (1519–1588), Thomas Bickley (1518–1596), and many others. Some of them were certainly helped by anonymous assistants.

Parker instructed the revisers to correct the Great Bible when it misrepresented the Hebrew and Greek texts, to consult the Latin translations of the Hebrew Bible done by Sanctes Pagninus in 1528 and Sebastian Münster in 1535, to adopt the Pagninus division into verses, and to stay away from polemics in their notes. Not all the scholars followed the Archbishops' recommendations. The depth of the revision varies from section to section. In the Apocrypha it is minimal, despite the fact that the Great Bible version of the Apocrypha had been based on the Latin Vulgate, not on the Greek original. The ban against controversial notes was respected. The verse division, on the other hand, was not taken from Pagninus, but followed the Geneva Bible.

Richard Jugge (d. 1577) spared no expense in printing the 1568 folio and produced the most beautiful sixteenth-century English Bible. He included a title page with a splendid portrait of Queen Elizabeth, five secondary title pages, 124 distinct woodcuts, and four maps (three of them borrowed from the Geneva Bible, one recycled from his own quarto Testaments of 1552–1566). He used his thickest paper in the New Testament knowing it would be read more often than the Old.[27] The Bible is open to show Elizabeth's portrait on its title page. William Cecil, the Queen's main advisor, is represented at the beginning of the Psalter in a cartouche that skillfully combines his portrait with the initial B in Psalm 1: *Blessed is the man …* (Fig. 8.1).

27. See Herbert 1968:125.

9. New Testament | Rheims: John Fogny, 1582

4°: [28], 745, [27] p.; 400 ff.; 180 x 129 mm. Herbert 177

10. Old Testament with Apocrypha | Douay: Laurence Kellam, 1609–1610

4°: vol. 1 †⁶ 2†⁴, A-6S⁴ 6T⁴; 568 ff. (signatures include w); vol. 2: A-6W⁴; 564 ff.; 180 x 134 mm. Herbert 300

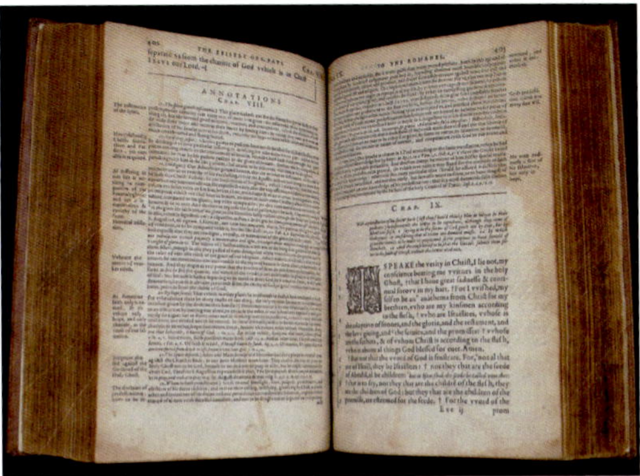

Fig. 9.1

After the accession of Elizabeth I it was the turn of the Catholic clergy to seek refuge on the Continent and organize the underground resistance to the established church. Many exiled scholars settled in the Spanish Low Countries, where Philip II had founded in 1559 a new Catholic university at Douay (also spelled Douai and, in English, Doway). Under the leadership of the future Cardinal William Allen (1532–1594) they opened in 1568 an English college and seminary at Douay and started training priests and missionaries that would go back to England and risk their lives trying to reinstate Catholicism there. Due to political pressure, the College moved to Rheims in 1578, but returned to Douay in 1593 and remained there for the next 200 years. It closed in 1793 in the wake of the French Revolution.[28]

The Douay exiles understood they needed their own English version of the Bible if they were to compete successfully against the Protestant preachers and spread the Catholic faith in Elizabeth's realm. Translating two chapters each day, Gregory Martin (c. 1540–1582) prepared a manuscript translation of the entire Bible in less than four years.[29] An Oxford scholar, Martin had specialized in Greek and Hebrew and was teaching the two languages at Rheims when he started translating the Bible. Nevertheless, he based his translation on the Latin Vulgate and defended the superiority of the Latin text in his Preface to his English version.[30] He made the valid point that Jerome's translation was based on fourth-century Greek manuscripts while the Greek texts available to his fellow scholars were based on late Byzantine sources. At the same time, he failed to recognize that the sixteenth-century text of the Vulgate was just as corrupt as the contemporary Greek Bibles.

Martin was assisted by several members of the English College including William Allen, Richard Bristow (1538–1581) and William Reynolds (1544–1594). Unidentified Douay scholars prepared the manuscript of the Old Testament for publication long after Martin's death. Barstow was probably the author of the most

28. For a short history of the University of Douay and its English College see *Catholic Encyclopedia* (1909 ed.) 5:138 and *New Catholic Encyclopedia* (1067 ed.) 5: 1020

29. He worked from October 1578 to March 1582, see Pollard 1911: 33 (= 21 in the facsimile edition)

30. See the Preface to the New Testament f. b3r and the Preface to the Old Testament f. †3v

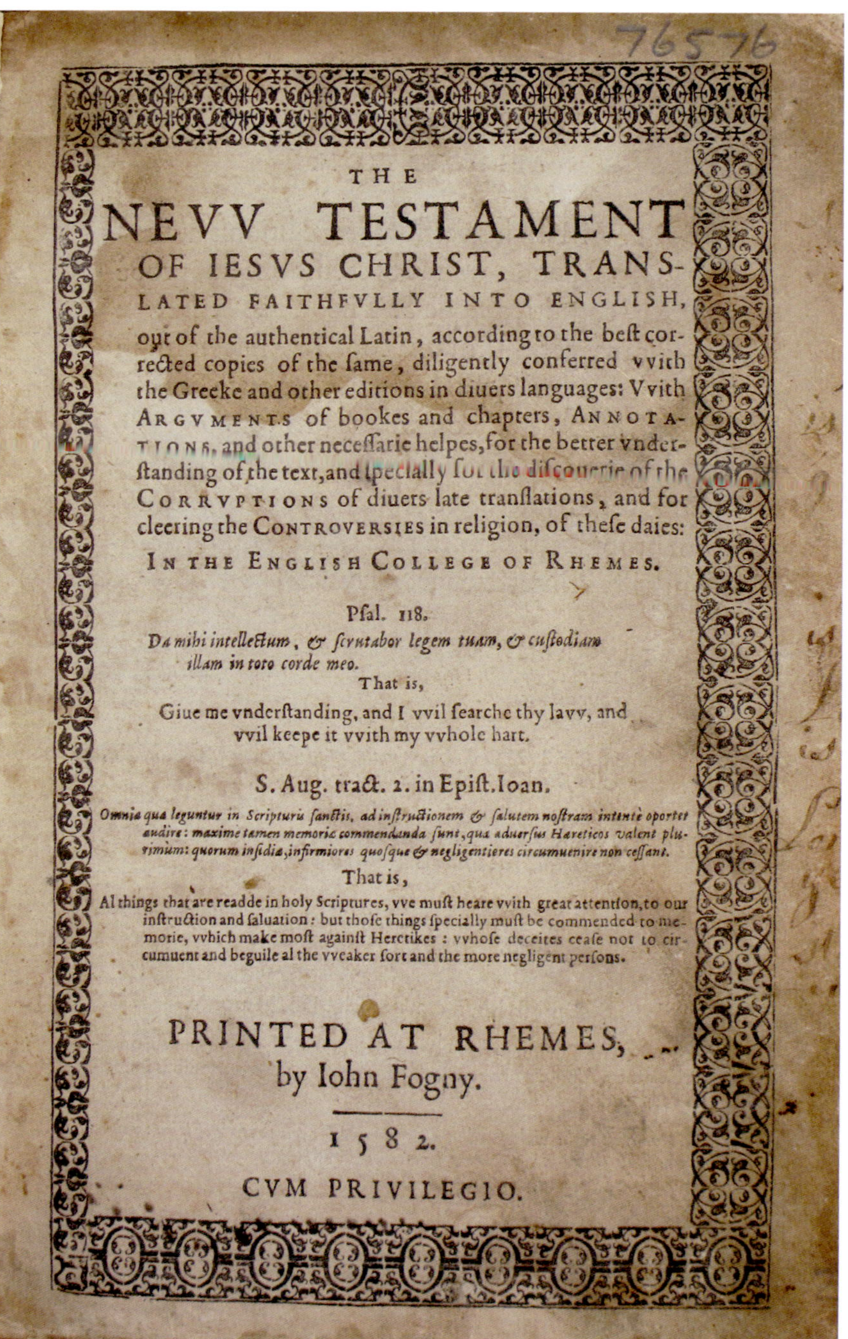

THE
NEVV TESTAMENT
OF IESVS CHRIST, TRANS-
LATED FAITHFVLLY INTO ENGLISH,

out of the authentical Latin, according to the best corrected copies of the same, diligently conferred vvith
the Greeke and other editions in diuers languages: Vvith
ARGVMENTS of bookes and chapters, ANNOTA-
TIONS, and other necessarie helpes, for the better vnderstanding of the text, and specially for the discouerie of the
CORRVPTIONS of diuers late translations, and for
cleering the CONTROVERSIES in religion, of these daies:

IN THE ENGLISH COLLEGE OF RHEMES.

Psal. 118.

Da mihi intellectum, & scrutabor legem tuam, & custodiam
illam in toto corde meo.

That is,

Giue me vnderstanding, and I vvil searche thy lavv, and
vvil keepe it vvith my vvhole hart.

S. Aug. tract. 2. in Epist. Ioan.

Omnia quæ leguntur in Scripturis sanctis, ad instructionem & salutem nostram intente oportet
audire: maxime tamen memoriæ commendanda sunt, quæ aduersus Hæreticos valent plu-
rimùm: quorum insidiæ, infirmiores quosque & negligentiores circumuenire non cessant.

That is,

Al things that are readde in holy Scriptures, vve must heare vvith great attention, to our
instruction and saluation: but those things specially must be commended to me-
morie, vvhich make most against Heretikes: vvhose deceites cease not to cir-
cumuent and beguile al the vveaker sort and the more negligent persons.

PRINTED AT RHEMES,
by Iohn Fogny.

1582.

CVM PRIVILEGIO.

9. New Testament

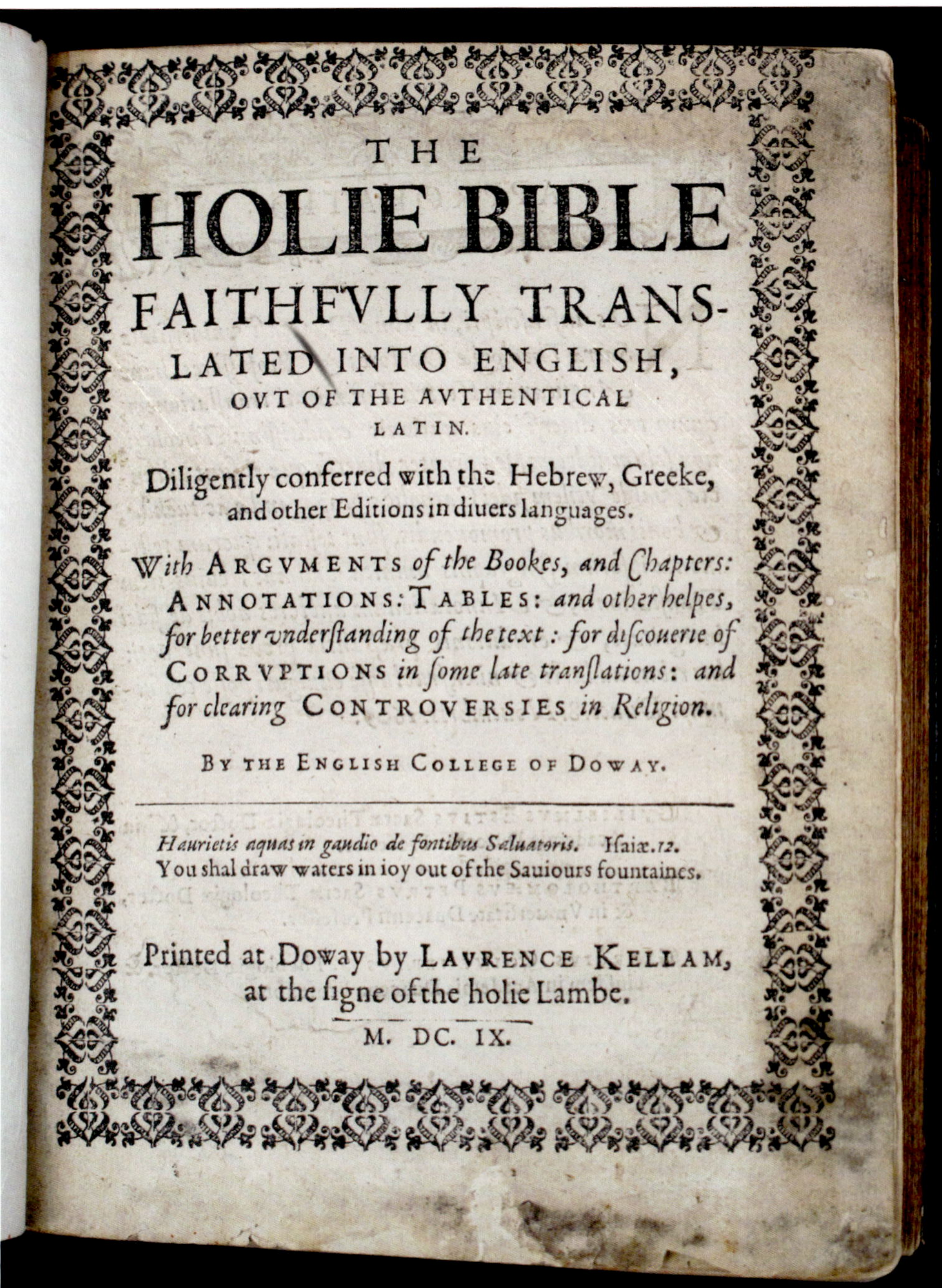

THE
HOLIE BIBLE

FAITHFVLLY TRANS-
LATED INTO ENGLISH,
OVT OF THE AVTHENTICAL
LATIN.

Diligently conferred with the Hebrew, Greeke,
and other Editions in diuers languages.

With ARGVMENTS of the Bookes, and Chapters:
ANNOTATIONS: TABLES: and other helpes,
for better vnderstanding of the text: for discouerie of
CORRVPTIONS in some late translations: and
for clearing CONTROVERSIES in Religion.

BY THE ENGLISH COLLEGE OF DOWAY.

Haurietis aquas in gaudio de fontibus Saluatoris. Isaiæ.12.
You shal draw waters in ioy out of the Sauiours fountaines.

Printed at Doway by LAVRENCE KELLAM,
at the signe of the holie Lambe.

M. DC. IX.

10. Old Testament with Apocrypha

controversial notes in the Catholic Bible. William Reynolds remained a devout Catholic and helped prepare the Rheims-Douay translation, while his younger brother John became a Puritan and joined the team that translated the King James Bible (see Ill. 2).

The title page of the 1582 edition of the New Testament lists all the important features of his work: it is a faithful translation of the Latin Vulgate, made with reference to the original languages and several modern translations, and it includes extensive notes meant to explain the text, reveal the errors of "divers late translations," and present the Catholic position in contemporary religious controversies.

Martin did consult the Greek and Hebrew texts and quoted them often in his marginal notes and chapter annotations.[31] His use of the definite article in the 1582 New Testament corresponds faithfully to the Greek text and cannot derive from the Vulgate since Latin has no articles. Like all translators, he also borrowed from the work of his predecessors: phrases taken from Tyndale, Coverdale or the Geneva Bible can be found in his version. At times, Martin imitated too closely the syntax and phrases of his Latin source and ended up writing barely intelligible English sentences.[32]

Martin's most enduring legacy is in the realm of English vocabulary, which he enriched with words of Latin and Greek origin. Nouns and verbs commonly used today such as *acquisition, character, cooperate, evangelize,* and *victim* go back to the Rheims New Testament. The translators of the King James Bible borrowed from the Catholic version a large number of words and phrases and may have contributed to their survival in literary English.[33] Interestingly, modern revisions of the King James Bible did not always retain the Latinisms of the 1611 edition. Words like *cure, deride,* and *fragments,* for instance, are replaced in the *New Revised Standard Version* by *heal, mock,* and *broken pieces.*

The publication of the Catholic translation took almost 30 years to complete. The New Testament was printed in 1582 by Jean de Fogny (1561–1593) in Rheims. The Old Testament was published almost 30 years later, in 1609–10, due to financial difficulties. Its printer was Laurence Kellam (d. 1614), who had worked at Louvain before moving to Douay in about 1603. The King James translators, who had ample time to study the Rheims New Testament, seem to have also known the first volume of the Douay Old Testament.

Both the New Testament and the first volume of the Old Testament are opened at their title pages. Fig. 9.1 shows Martin's annotations to Romans 8.

31. See, for instance, Preface to the New Testament f. c4r and Old Testament p. 57

32. Daniell 2003:363 quotes 1Co 5:7 *that you may be a new paste as you are Azymes,* Eph 3:6 *concorporat and comparticipant,* and 2Pe 2:13 *conquinations and spots flowing in delicacies*

33. See the impressive lists compiled by Carleton 1902

II. Birth of a Masterpiece

The making of the King James Bible is documented in a variety of sources that allow us to follow its history from the moment of its conception at the Hampton Court Conference, in January 1604, to its final revision in 1610. No comparable evidence exists for any other English translation done before the twentieth century. While there are still gaps in our knowledge and part of the information may have been lost forever, the main lines of the story can be defined with reasonable clarity. The persons involved in this story are King James and his fifty-odd translators. The tools they used are editions of the Bible in English, Hebrew, Greek, and other languages, standard reference books, and a common set of rules and procedures that helped organize both the initial work and its multiple revisions.

The Hampton Court Conference

In April 1603, the Puritan ministers who felt that the Reformation had not gone far enough in Tudor England presented to James I a document said to bear 1,000 signatures and hence known as the Millenary Petition. They were expressing their dissatisfaction with the Anglican Church and the Roman Catholic practices still used in its ritual or mentioned in its prayer book. They clearly expected that James, who had been raised in Presbyterian Scotland, would suppress any trace of popery. James answered by summoning to his Hampton Court Palace the elite of the established Church, including Archbishop Whitgift, eight bishops, and seven deans, and four Puritans known as scholarly and moderate. A three-day long conference was held on January 14, 16, and 18, 1604. The same year, William Barlow, the Dean of Chester, published the only official account of its proceedings.[34]

34. See also Curtis in Burke 2009: 57–71

contempt of his Maiesties Proclamation made for the reforming of that abuse, of which hee earnestly desired a straighter course for reformation thereof, and to this he found a general and vnanimous assent.

After that, he moued his Maiestie, that there might bee a newe *translation* of the *Bible*, because, those which were allowed in the raignes of *Henrie* the eight, and *Edward* the sixt, were corrupt and not aunswerable to the truth of the Originall. For example, first, *Galathians*, 4. 25. the Greeke worde συσιχει, is not well translated, as nowe it is, *Bordreth*, neither expressing the force of the worde, nor the Apostles sense, nor the situation of the place.

Secondly, *Psalme*, 105. 28. *they were not obedient*; The Originall beeing, *They were not disobedient.*

Thirdly, *Psalme*, 106. verse 30. Then stood vp *Phinees* and *prayed*, the Hebrew hath *Executed iudgement*. To which
G 3   motion,

11. William Barlow

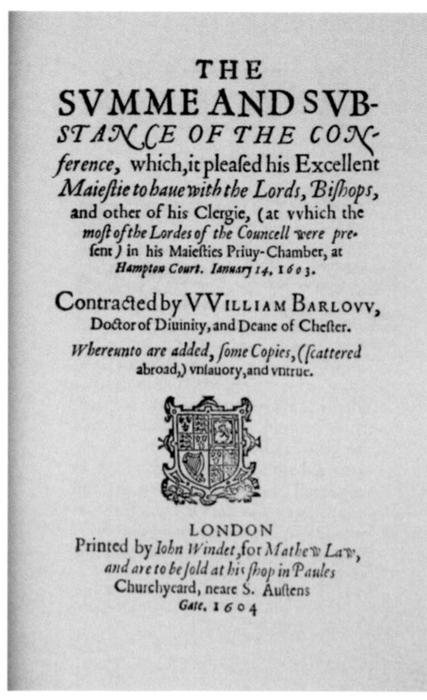

Fig. 11.1

William Barlow was one of the participants in the Conference held at Hampton Court in January 1604 and his eyewitness account was published before the end of the year, when the event was still fresh in his memory and other colleagues could challenge his recollection. Barlow's memoir was widely circulated in England and was also translated into French. No fewer than five editions of the text were produced in 1604 and 1605: two in English and three in French. Unofficial accounts of the Conference, described by Barlow as "unsavory and untrue," were also issued in 1604 and scattered comments made by other participants survive in various documents.[35] Set against such contemporary evidence, Barlow's narrative appears essentially credible.[36] It is also clear, however, that he toned down some of James' petulant outbursts and failed to record at least one unpleasant incident.

The King rejected most of the Puritans' requests. We can only sympathize with John Reynolds, their spokesman, who day after day kneeled before James and addressed his royal person only to be refuted and rebuked. On the second day of the conference, however, the Puritan scholar scored a small victory when the King received favorably his objections to the short catechism included in the *Book of Common Prayer* and there was "general and unanimous assent" for his views on the profanation of the Sabbath. Maybe encouraged by these successes, Reynolds unexpectedly asked the King "that there may be a new translation of the Bible."[37] He argued that the Bibles published during the reigns of Henry VIII and Edward VI were full of mistakes and misrepresented the original texts. Four versions had circulated during that period: Tyndale's, Coverdale's, Matthew's and the Great Bible. The Geneva Bible, translated by Puritan exiles in 1560, and the Bishops' Bible, issued in 1568 dated from Elizabeth's reign and did not fall under Reynolds' sweeping criticism. Reynolds certainly preferred the Geneva Bible to all other English versions and he probably envisioned the new translation as an exalted

35. Nicolson 2003: 54, 57

36. For a different opinion see Daniell 2003: 432–435

37. Barlow 1604:45

form of the Puritan edition. Unexpectedly, James assented to his proposal, but he also declared his contempt for the Geneva Bible and dismissed it as the "worst of all" English translations.[38] In retrospect, approving the idea of a new Bible translation was the most important decision King James ever made and provided the only enduring monument to his name. The King James Bible was conceived in that fateful instant. Some of the bishops and most of the scholars summoned to Hampton Court were going to be its translators. For the king, the new translation was an important means to consolidate religious unity and peace through the realm.

The facsimile edition of Barlow's account, open to page 45, shows the first mention of a new translation. Fig. 11.1 is a photograph of the book's title page.

King and Translators

James Stuart became King of Scotland in July 1567, when he was 13 months old, and inherited the throne of England upon the death of Elizabeth I, in March 1603. He was educated by stern tutors, including the humanist George Buchanan (1506–1582), who instilled in him a love of literature and learning and a passion for theological disputation. A firm believer in the divine right of kings, James supported the ecclesiastical hierarchy and distrusted the Puritans. He was the only British monarch to have his collected works published. James's editor was one of the Bible Translators, James Montagu (*c.* 1568–1618), who produced an English version of James' Latin texts and had them published in 1616 in London. Not surprisingly, a Latin version of the book was reprinted several times before the King's death in 1625.

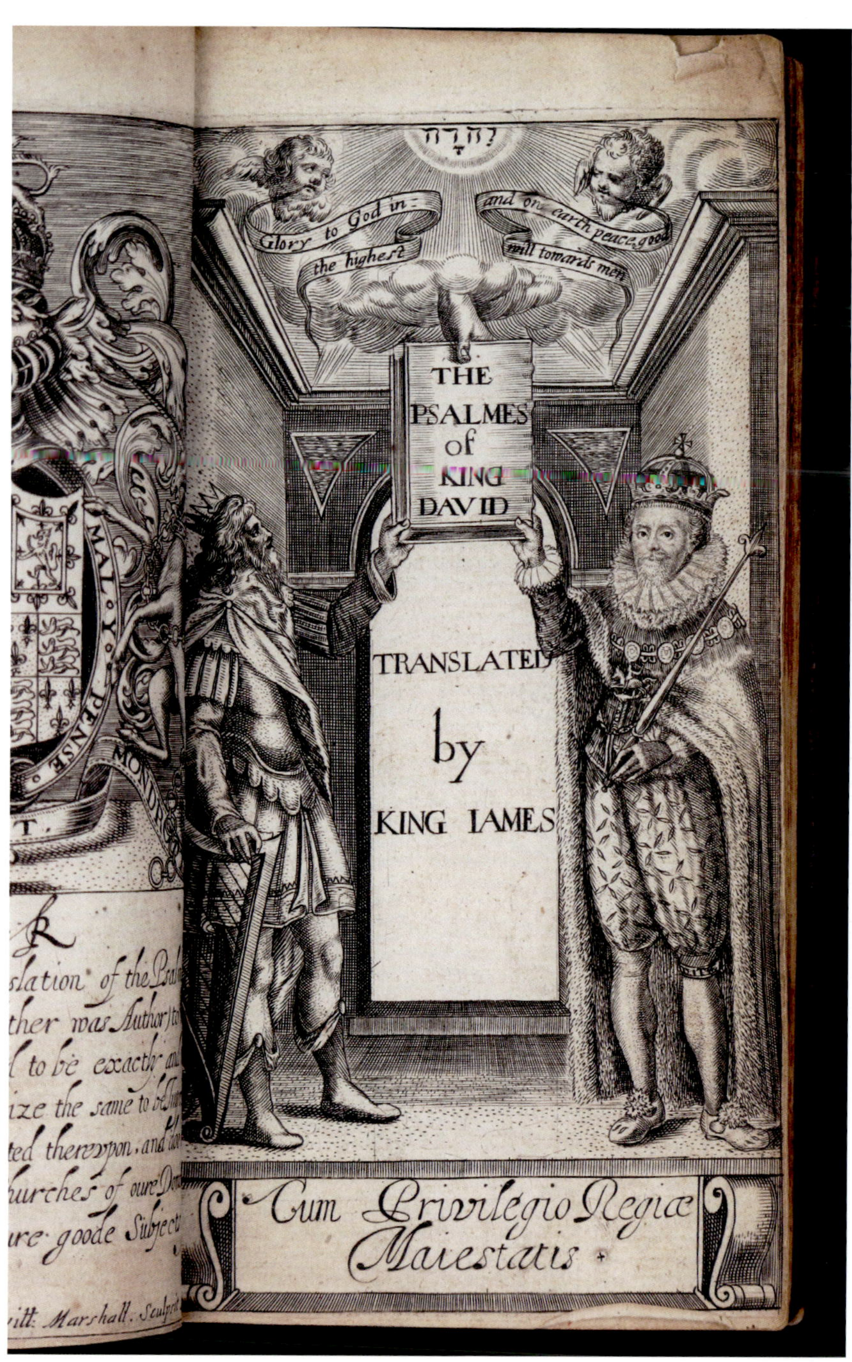

12. Metrical Psalms in English

OXFORD: WILLIAM TURNER, 1631

12mo: [4], 319, [1] p.; [π] ² A-N¹² O⁴; 162 ff.; 145 mm.

In 1631, James' son and heir, Charles I, authorized the publication of a verse translation of the Psalms attributed to his "late dear father" and allowed the text to be sung in all churches. The translation was reprinted in London, in 1636 and 1637, but did not become popular and failed to replace the standard collection of metrical Psalms put together by Thomas Sternhold and John Hopkins in 1562. The extent of King James' contribution to the 1631 text is hard to determine, but it appears that most of the work was done by William Alexander (*c.* 1570–1640), a Scottish poet who had followed the King to London after 1603 and was made Earl of Stirling in 1614.

Ironically, the Bible associated with King James does not depict the monarch on its title page while the Great Bible has an image of Henry VIII and the Bishops' Bible, a portrait of Elizabeth (see Cats. 6 and 8). James' portrait was included instead in this posthumous edition of the Psalms. On its title page, shown here, King James in full regalia faces the reader while to his right King David, his counterpart, is holding his harp and looking upwards for divine inspiration. The image was created by the engraver William Marshall (active 1617–1649), best remembered today for his representation of Charles I as a Christian martyr in a book titled *Eikon Basilike* ("Royal Portrait") that was published on February 9, 1649, ten days after Charles' execution.

Several contemporary oil portraits of King James survive, including one by Daniel Mytens (or Mijtens, *c.* 1590–1647/48), a Dutch artist who also painted his son Charles I, and copied older portraits of their royal ancestors (Ill. 1). Mytens represented James wearing the insignia of the Order of the Garter against the backdrop of a tapestry that includes the Tudor rose and the sitter's motto *Beati Pacifici* ("blessed are the peace makers") taken from the Latin version of the Sermon on the Mount (Matthew 5:9).

King James' Translators (the word was spelled with a capital T at the time[39]) were scholars with high status in the ecclesiastical hierarchy and the academic world and left substantial traces in the written accounts of the era and its gallery of portraits. For many of them we have detailed biographies as well as engravings and even oil paintings. A few are mentioned here as a preface to a more detailed discussion of their work.

John Reynolds (or Rainolds, 1549–1607) was one of the four Puritan ministers invited to the Hampton Court Conference and the spokesman for the entire group. He introduced the proposal that led to the publication of the King James Bible and was a member of the First Oxford Company, whose task was to translate the Prophetic Books (Isaiah to Malachi). According to a history of Oxford University compiled by Anthony Wood in the late 1660s, Reynolds hosted

39. Nicolson 2003: 42

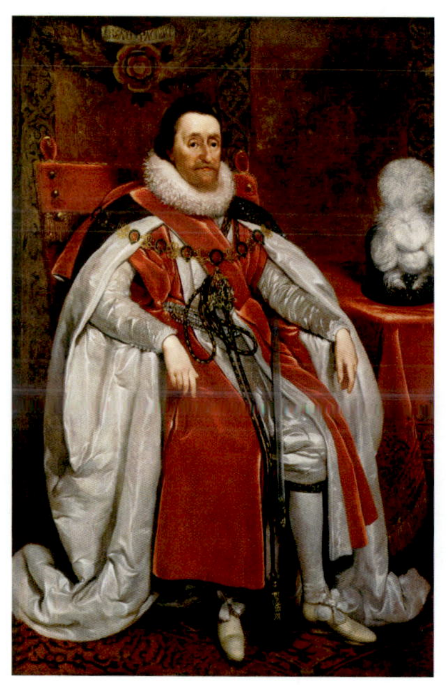

Ill. 1

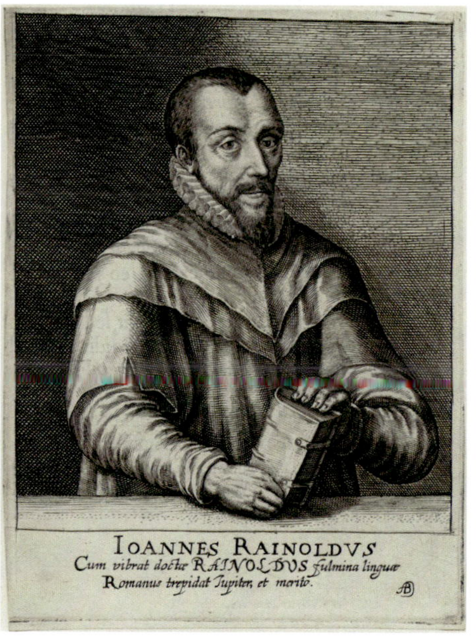

Ill. 2

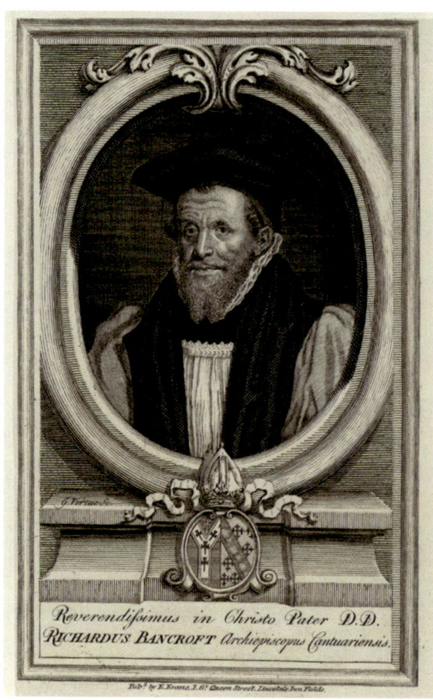

Ill. 3

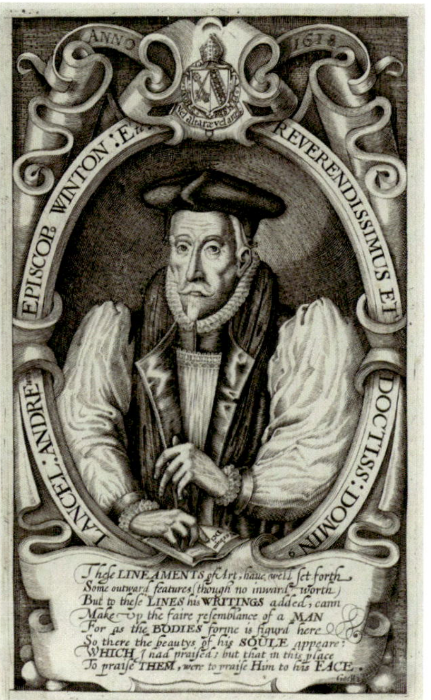

Ill. 4

the weekly meetings of his Company and was its most active Translator despite
being "sorely afflicted with gout."[40] Death prevented him from working on the final
revision of the text and seeing the completed printed Bible.

40. Nicolson 2004: 148

Reynolds' only surviving portrait (Ill. 2) was engraved after his death. The
work is attributed to one of the de Passe siblings, either Magdalena (1600–1638)
or her elder brother Willem (1598–c. 1637). Several members of this well-known
family of engravers had worked for the English market. Appropriately for an
Oxford scholar, Reynolds is represented holding a book, probably a copy of his
original writings. The Latin inscription at the bottom of the image mentions the
thunderbolts of his eloquence.

Richard Bancroft (1544–1610) attended the Hampton Court Conference in
January 1604 as Bishop of London. Ten months later, in November 1604, he was
enthroned Archbishop of Canterbury. During the Conference he opposed strongly
the idea of a new translation of the Bible, but once the King approved it, he worked
relentlessly to gather a team of Translators and organize their work. He selected
the best scholars and the most able writers regardless of their church affiliation.
Bancroft defined the rules and procedures they were to follow and generally acted
as liaison between the King and his Translators. Like Reynolds, he died before the
Bible was published.

Bancroft's portrait (Ill. 3) was executed in 1745 by George Vertue (1684–
1756), a prolific and talented engraver and antiquarian, based on an earlier
anonymous oil painting. The exact date of the painting is unknown, but it has to
be after 1604 since the portrait shows Bancroft as Archbishop of Canterbury.

Lancelot Andrewes (1555–1626), the Dean of Westminster, was the President
of the First Company of Translators responsible for the first half of the Old
Testament, from Genesis to 2 Kings. He worked with a group of brilliant scholars
with conservative Protestant backgrounds. He was chaplain to both Elizabeth and
James, who greatly admired his sermons. An indefatigable worker, he pushed his
team and complained that most of his colleagues were negligent.[41] James furthered
his career and made him Bishop of Chichester in 1605, Bishop of Ely in 1609, and
Bishop of Winchester in 1618, the year he attended the Synod of Dort. The prelates
of England had sent the Synod a Latin document about the making of the King
James Bible.

41 Nicolson 2003: 192

This portrait of Lancelot Andrewes (Ill. 4) commemorates his elevation
to the See of Winchester and includes a short poem in English that praises his
writings without mentioning the Bible translation. It was engraved by Simon de
Passe (c. 1595–1647), eldest brother of Magdalena and Willem to whom the portrait
of John Reynolds is attributed. Simon had settled in London in 1616 and was a very

44. See Norton 2005: 6–11;
Nicolson 2003: 71–83

Ill. 7

To coordinate the work of this huge team of scholars, Bancroft issued a set of written instructions that define some general principles and describe specific procedures (Ill. 7). The document, known through four slightly different manuscript copies, can be considered the first handbook for Bible translators.[44] The ultimate authority of the Hebrew and Greek texts is recognized in the first of the 15 rules devised by Bancroft and sanctioned by the King. The importance of Patristic literature for clarifying obscure passages and the authority of Church tradition ("the Ancient Fathers … and the Analogy of Faith") are upheld in Rule 4. Rule 14, which is the last one in two of the manuscripts, lists the English versions to be considered by the Translators in addition to the Bishops' Bible already mentioned in Rule 1. Bancroft's list includes all the printed translations of the English Bible with the significant omission of the Catholic version of the New Testament published in Rheims in 1582 (see Cat. 9).

Conservative solutions are recommended more than once: in the area of ecclesiastical vocabulary, the older equivalents are to be maintained (*Church* rather than *Congregation* specifies Rule 3); the personal names in the Bible should retain their familiar English form; the division into chapters should be altered as little as possible.

Three simple words at the beginning of Rule 6 had immense consequences for the acceptance of the King James Bible: *No marginal notes.* The bare text of the Translators did not generate the controversies that had plagued the annotated editions of the Geneva and Rheims-Douay versions. Over the centuries, the absence of sectarian comments encouraged a large spectrum of Protestant churches to appropriate the King James Bible as their own version. Short technical notes did not fall under Bancroft's interdict. The Translators were encouraged to gloss on the meaning of Hebrew or Greek words that have no single-word equivalent in English and to establish a system of cross-references among similar or identical biblical texts.

Last, but by no means least, Bancroft's rules made detailed provisions for a multi-level system of translating, checking and revising. Initially, the members of each Company were to translate separately the same text, then meet to discuss their work and produce a common first draft; that draft was to be

circulated among all the other Companies who were to "consider" it "seriously
and judiciously;" a general meeting would then be called to arbitrate in case of
disagreement between the Companies; finally a committee including the heads of
each of the Companies and a few theologians not involved in the project was to
make a last revision.

THE COMPANIES AT WORK

The first of the rules given to the Translators instructed them to follow the
wording of the Bishops' Bible (see Cat. 8) as closely as possible and alter it only
in the interest of conformity to the original Hebrew and Greek texts. The edition
they used was the 1602 folio printed by Richard Barker. The printer supplied for
the Translators 40 unbound copies of this folio and submitted a bill dating from
May 10, 1605.[45] A copy of the 1602 Bishops' Bible that has no connection to the
Translators is displayed in this *On Eagles' Wings*.

45. See Norton 2005:12
and note 16

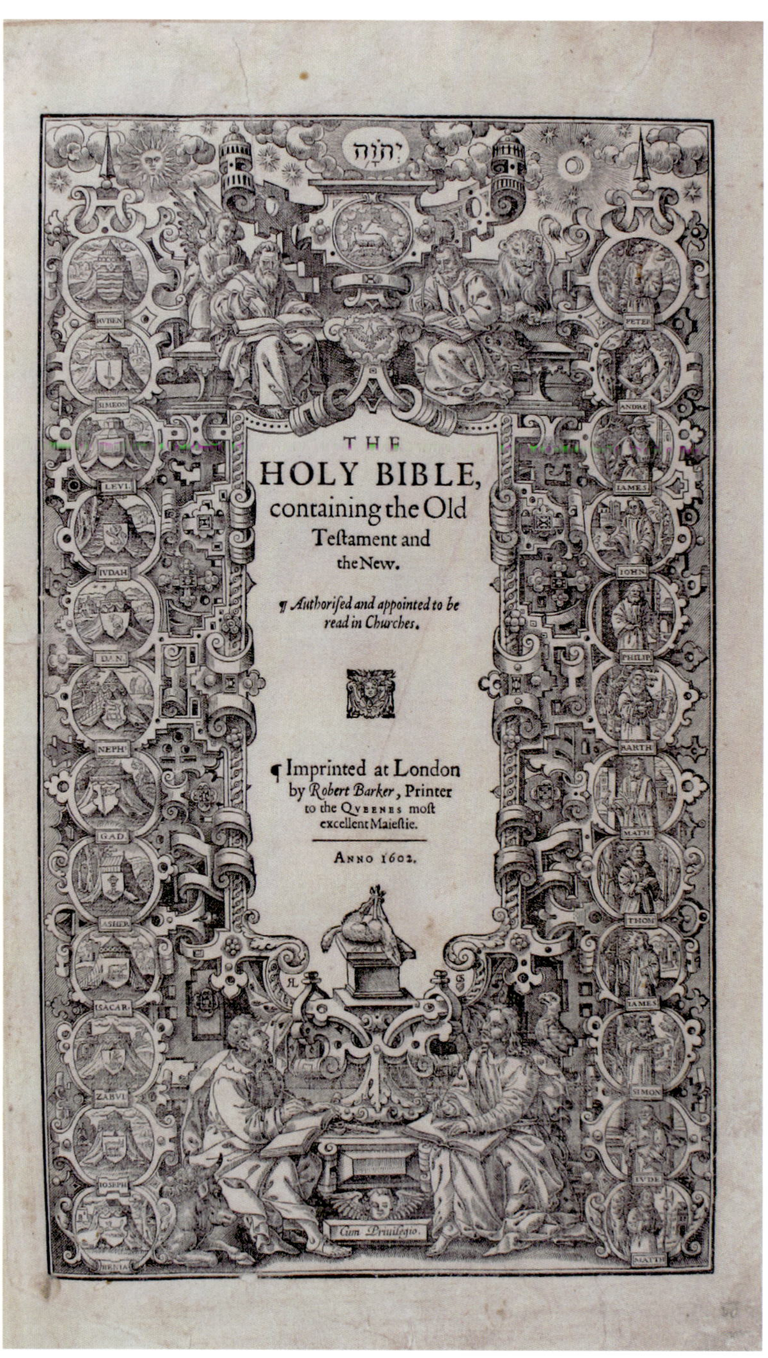

13. Bible with Apocrypha

The Bishops' Bible had been printed by Richard Jugge between 1568 and 1577, by Christopher Barker between 1578 and 1598, and by Robert Barker, Christopher's son and the future printer of the King James Bible, in 1602. Separate editions of the New Testament in the Bishops' version were published sporadically until 1633, but the 1602 folio was the last edition of the complete Bible. In passing from one printer to the other the biblical text remained essentially the same, but the number of illustrations was drastically reduced. Jugge's 1568 folio has four maps and numerous woodcuts printed from 124 distinct blocks, while Robert Barker's 1602 Bible has only one engraving.

In the first edition of the Bishops' Bible the preface written by its principal editor, Archbishop Matthew Parker (1504–1575), was followed by a reprint of the preface prepared by Archbishop Thomas Cranmer (1489–1556) for the 1540 edition of the Great Bible. Starting in 1584, Christopher Barker dropped Parker's preface from all his editions of the Bishops' text and Cranmer's preface from half of them. Robert Barker reinstated Cranmer's text in his 1602 folio "at the request of divers learned," in consideration of its utility and excellence, and to honor the memory of the prelate who had been martyred by Queen Mary in 1556.

Robert Barker corrected some of the misprints of the earlier editions and added new errors of his own. Some of the errors proper to the 1602 edition have found their way into the 1611 King James Bible providing additional proof that it was indeed the edition used by the Jacobean Translators. Two of the examples cited by Norton[46] are particularly clear: in 1 Kings 8:61, the 1568 Bishops' Bible has the correct reading *the Lord our God* while the 1602 and the 1611 share the erroneous *the Lord your God* and in 1 Kings 11:5 the 1568 edition correctly reads *Ammonites* while the 1602 and 1611 editions read *Amorites*. According to Norton, the first edition of the King James Bible has taken from the 1602 folio some 250 readings.

The title page of the 1602 folio, shown here, includes the Tetragrammaton and the slain lamb on the altar, the four Evangelists, the tents of the 12 tribes of Israel, and the 12 Apostles. Barker reused it as the secondary title page in some copies of the first edition of the King James Bible (see Cat. 16).

In addition to the Bishops' Bible and the earlier English translations described in the first section of this catalog, the translators certainly used all the standard tools of their trade: printed editions of the Hebrew Bible and Greek New Testament, an assortment of grammars and dictionaries, and a variety of Bible translations into Latin, Syriac, and the major languages of Europe. While it is both inadvisable and impossible to replicate the holdings of their libraries, one Hebrew and one Greek text will illustrate the main sources of their work.

46. 2005: 36

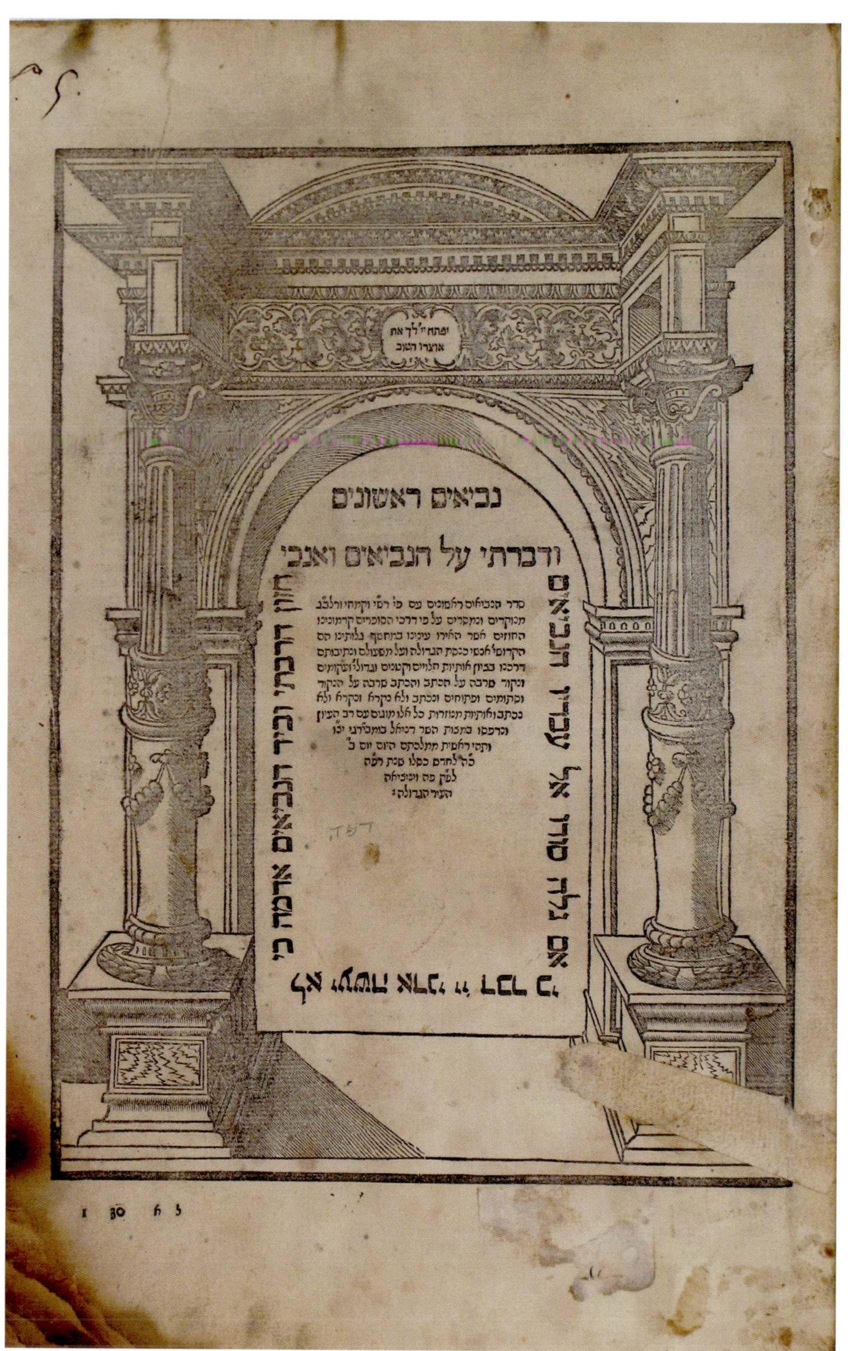

14. Hebrew Bible

Venice: Daniel Bomberg, 1524–25

Vol. 2: Joshua, Judges, 1–2 Samuel, 1–2 Kings; 21 November 1524

2°: 30–54⁸ 55¹⁰; 210 ff. 335 x 195 mm. DM 5085

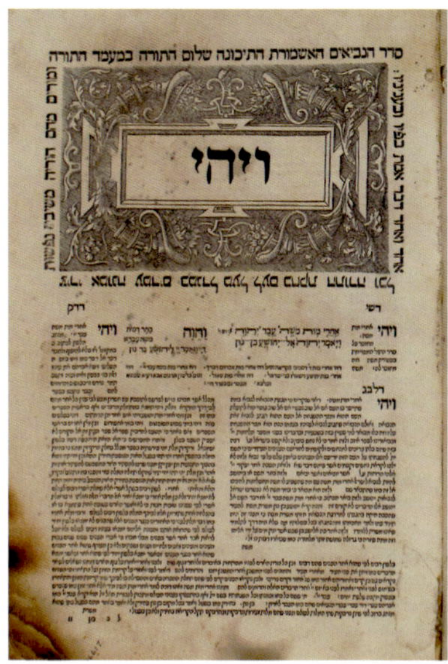

Fig. 14.1

Printing in Hebrew character started in the 1470s and by the end of the fifteenth century 36 editions of the Hebrew Bible issued in its entirety or in separate parts had been produced. Daniel Bomberg (d. 1549/1553) was the first Christian publisher of Hebrew books. His first Hebrew Bible, printed in Venice in 1517–18 and edited by Felix Pratensis, a converted Jew (d. 1539), was not well received in the Jewish communities. For his second edition of the Bible, Bomberg enlisted the help of his proofreader, Jacob b. Hayyim (*c.* 1470–*c.* 1538), who revised the 1517 text using Sephardic manuscripts, wrote a detailed introduction to the four-volume set, and added to the standard rabbinic commentaries a clearly edited version of the Masorah. The text of Bomberg's second *Biblia Rabbinica* soon came to be considered the standard Masoretic text of the Hebrew Bible and was the source of countless editions until the early twentieth century.

Undoubtedly the Jacobean Translators used editions of the Hebrew Bible that derived from Bomberg's text. They probably also consulted the first four volumes of the Complutensian Polyglot[47] and the new Latin translations of the Old Testament published during the sixteenth century. In his preface to the King James Bible, Miles Smith mentions Sanctes Pagninus, the author of a Latin version first published in 1528. A different Latin translation prepared by Immanuel Tremellius and his son-in-law Franciscus Junius was printed in Frankfurt am Main in 1577–79. Scrivener has proved that many marginal notes in the 1611 Bible are based on a revised edition of the Tremellius-Junius Latin version published in London in 1593.[48]

The Bible's second volume is open to show its title page. Fig. 14.1 shows the first page of Joshua with the biblical text surrounded by rabbinic commentaries.

47. See Scrivener 1884: 42–43

48. Scrivener 1884: 44

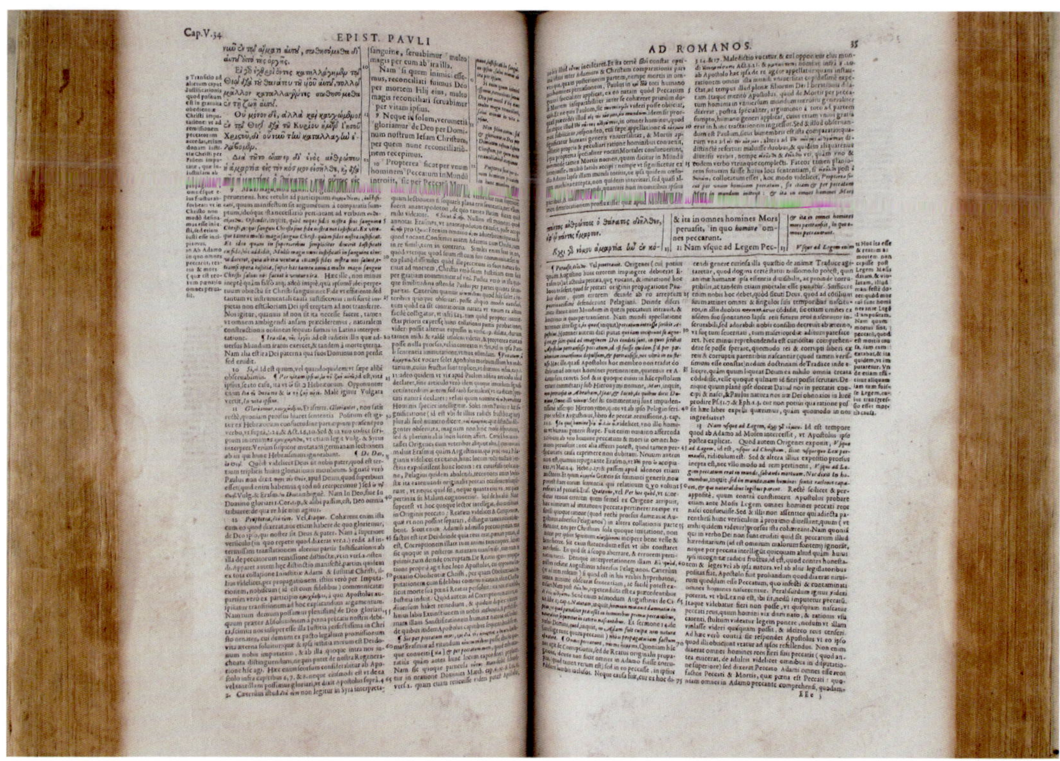

15. New Testament in Greek and Latin

[GENEVA]: HEIRS OF EUSTACHE VIGNON, 1598

2°: ¶⁴ a-b⁶ 2A-5A⁶ 5B⁸ 5C-5D⁶; 456 ff.; 1-577, 1–563 p.; 280 x 160 mm. DM 4654, WLB C165

Like all their contemporaries, the Jacobean Translators read the Greek New Testament in printed editions based on late Byzantine manuscripts. In the early 1600s the three earliest manuscripts of the text known today were unavailable in Western Europe: the Codex Alexandrinus arrived in England in 1627, the Codex Vaticanus was first collated in 1669, and the Codex Sinaiticus was discovered only in 1844. Théodore de Bèze (1519–1605), known as Beza in the international community, had sent to Cambridge in 1581 a fifth-century manuscript of the Gospels and Acts in Greek and Latin, but his cover letter contained a serious caveat: the codex should be preserved rather than used since many persons "may find offensive the depravity of its text."[49] It is no wonder the manuscript was ignored for the next two centuries.

49. See the Preface to the photographic edition published by Cambridge University Press in 1899

Printed editions of the Greek New Testament were first issued in the 1510s. The Complutensian text edited by Demetrios Ducas (*c.* 1480–*c.* 1527) based on two manuscripts borrowed from the Vatican Library, left the printer's shop on January 10, 1514, but did not reach the scholarly community until December 1521. Erasmus' text, based on more recent manuscripts, though printed later than the Complutensian, became available in March 1516 and was far more popular than the Spanish edition. The 1516 text was revised by Erasmus himself between 1518 and 1527, by Robert Estienne (also known as Stephanus) in 1546 and 1550, and by Beza starting in 1565. The Translators of the King James Bible were familiar with all the main editions of the Greek New Testament. Their influence can be detected behind the wording of the 1611 English text, in its marginal annotations, and, sometimes, in John Bois' handwritten notes.[50] The Greek text they followed most frequently was Beza's. By the 1630s, this text was being reprinted throughout Western Europe and was generally known as the *textus receptus,* "the received text."

50. Scrivener 1884: 243–263; Allen 1969: 94–95, 122, 124. See also Ill. 8

A follower of Calvin, Beza was one of the most learned theologians of his time. He spent the last four decades of his life in Geneva as professor of Greek and Theology and became the leader of the Swiss Reformed Church after Calvin's death in 1564. Beza published his first edition of the Greek New Testament in 1565 and continued to revise and refine his work until 1598. During this period, he issued four folio or major editions with extensive commentaries and four small-size or minor editions with marginal notes. John Bois repeatedly quoted Beza's comments in the fourth major edition and the other Translators probably used it as well.

Beza's monumental last edition includes in three parallel columns the Greek text, his own Latin translation, and the standard Latin text of the Vulgate. Cross-references and short explanatory notes are printed in the margin, while an ample and quite erudite commentary is placed at the bottom of the page. In the Pauline Epistles, this commentary takes most of the space in each page. In Romans 5: 10–13, the text shown here, Beza fills almost completely two folio pages while explaining only six lines of standard Greek text. The remarks on the words he translated as *in quo [homine],* "in whom," at the end of Romans v. 12 are quoted literally in Bois' notes (see Ill. 8). They were added in the fourth edition only and are the source of the marginal note in the 1611 English text.

The fifty-odd Translators had already been selected by July 1604 and some groups began working before the end of the year. It took the six Companies about three years to complete the first stage of their task. By the beginning of 1608 many Companies, if not all of them, had finished their first drafts of the translation and were circulating them among the other groups. A manuscript preserved in Lambeth Palace (MS 98) has a draft text of the New Testament Epistles in the left column and a blank right column. The Second Westminster Company probably meant to circulate it among the five other groups and provided a space for their comments and suggestions.[51] The manuscript is an indirect witness to the first stage of the revision process.

51. Norton 2005: 15 quoting a study by Allen

In December 1608, King James sent the Archbishop of Canterbury a letter ordering the Translators to complete the Bible as soon as possible. Following the royal command, the "general meeting" stipulated in Rule 10 was convened to finalize the text of the translation. A committee including probably 12 members (two for each Company) met in the Hall of the Stationers' Company in London for a period of nine months in 1609–10. Each reviser received from the Stationers' Company 30 shillings a week. Only one of them took notes during the meetings: John Bois. Bois' autograph manuscript is now lost, but his notes on the Epistles and Revelation survive in a copy made by William Fulman (1632–1688), a much younger Oxford friend of Bois' who bequeathed all his papers to Corpus Christi College (Ill. 8). Ward Allen, the first scholar to identify and study Fulman's copy of Bois' notes, published in 1969 a scholarly edition of the manuscript. For the modern reader's convenience, he translated both the Greek and the Latin phrases in the original manuscript and transcribed in italics its English text.

Strange as it may seem today, Bois' notes are written in Latin. They include quotations from the Greek text and explore alternative ways of rendering it in English, but the language frame of the entire discourse is definitely Latin. Bois' notes bring before our eyes 12 learned men discussing in Latin the niceties of a Greek text and the best way to translate it in English. Bois' note to Romans 5:12, included in the document shown here (Ills. 8 and 8.1) contains a quote from the Greek New Testament edited by Beza in 1598 (see Cat. 15) and found its way into the marginal notes of the King James Bible. Many other quotations from various sources, including Chrysostom and Tertullian, are scattered through Bois' notes and reveal the depth and breadth of his scholarship, his familiarity with Patristic literature and his willingness to adopt the practice recommended in Rule 4.

One of the 40 copies of the 1602 Bishops' Bible provided by Robert Barker for the Translators survives and is an important witness to the work of the revisers of the King James text. Its margins are covered with handwritten notes that account for many, although not all, of the differences between the 1602 text and the editions printed in 1611. The Bodleian Library in Oxford acquired it in 1646 for 13 shillings and 4 pence and cataloged it as "a large Bible wherein is written down all the Alterations in the last translation."[52] The annotations in the Bodleian copy of the 1602 Bible testify to a text that is closer to the printed editions than any other existing document. The Bodleian copy is neither the master copy sent to the printers nor an exact replica of the master copy. However, it allows us to witness the transmutation of the pedestrian text of the 1602 Bible into the perennial masterpiece produced by the Jacobean Translators. In Genesis 1:6, for instance, the 1602 Bible reads:

52. Nicolson 2003:151

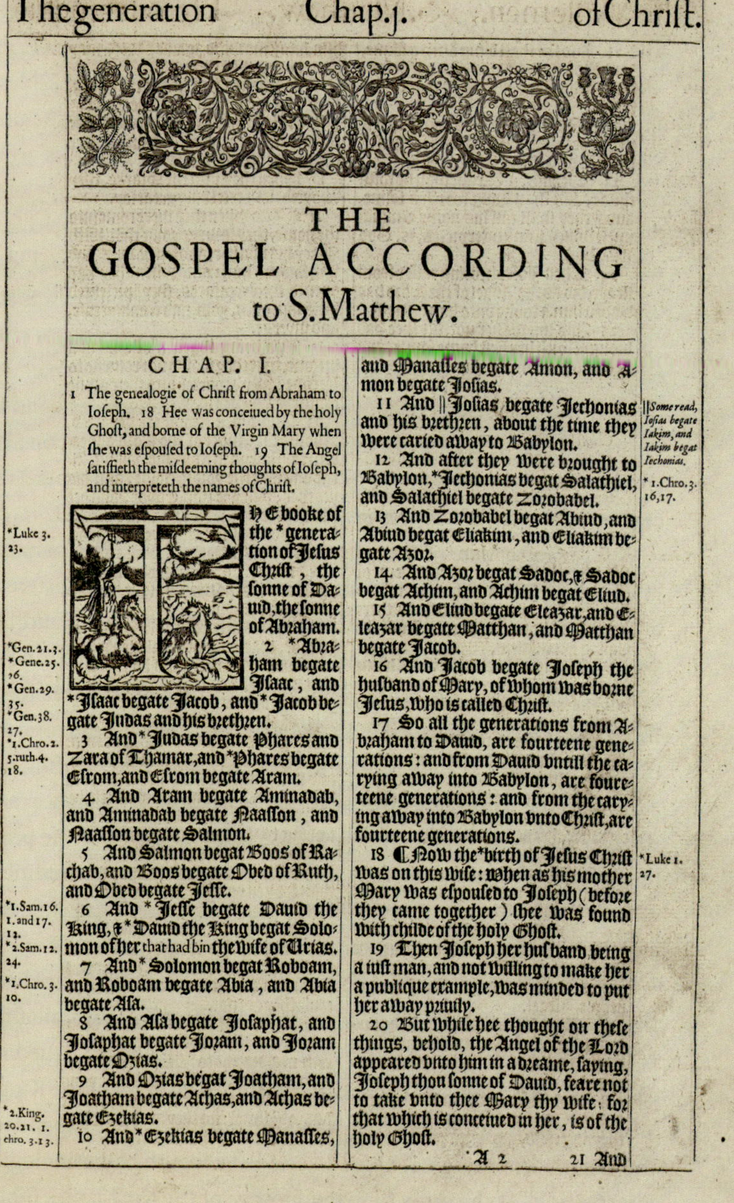

THE
GOSPEL ACCORDING
to S.Matthew.

CHAP. I.

1 The genealogie of Christ from Abraham to Ioseph. 18 Hee was conceiued by the holy Ghost, and borne of the Virgin Mary when she was espoused to Ioseph. 19 The Angel satisfieth the misdeeming thoughts of Ioseph, and interpreteth the names of Christ.

*Luke 3. 23.

*Gen. 21. 3.
*Gene. 25. 26.
*Gen. 29. 35.
*Gen. 38. 27.
*1.Chro. 2. 5. ruth. 4. 18.

HE booke of the *generation of Iesus Christ, the sonne of Dauid, the sonne of Abraham.

2 *Abraham begate Isaac, and *Isaac begate Iacob, and *Iacob begate Iudas and his brethren.

3 And *Iudas begate Phares and Zara of Thamar, and *Phares begate Esrom, and Esrom begate Aram.

4 And Aram begate Aminadab, and Aminadab begate Naasson, and Naasson begate Salmon.

5 And Salmon begat Boos of Rachab, and Boos begate Obed of Ruth, and Obed begate Iesse.

*1.Sam. 16. 1. and 17. 12.
*2.Sam. 12. 24.
*1.Chro. 3. 10.

6 And *Iesse begate Dauid the King, & *Dauid the King begat Solomon of her that had bin the wife of Urias.

7 And *Solomon begat Roboam, and Roboam begate Abia, and Abia begate Asa.

8 And Asa begate Iosaphat, and Iosaphat begate Ioram, and Ioram begate Ozias.

*2.King. 20. 21. 1. chro. 3. 13.

9 And Ozias begat Ioatham, and Ioatham begate Achas, and Achas begate Ezekias.

10 And *Ezekias begate Manasses, and Manasses begate Amon, and Amon begate Iosias.

11 And ‖ Iosias begate Iechonias and his brethren, about the time they were caried away to Babylon.

12 And after they were brought to Babylon, *Iechonias begat Salathiel, and Salathiel begate Zorobabel.

13 And Zorobabel begat Abiud, and Abiud begat Eliakim, and Eliakim begate Azor.

14 And Azor begat Sadoc, & Sadoc begat Achim, and Achim begat Eliud.

15 And Eliud begate Eleazar, and Eleazar begate Matthan, and Matthan begate Iacob.

16 And Iacob begate Ioseph the husband of Mary, of whom was borne Iesus, who is called Christ.

17 So all the generations from Abraham to Dauid, are fourteene generations: and from Dauid vntill the carying away into Babylon, are fourteene generations: and from the carying away into Babylon vnto Christ, are fourteene generations.

‖ Some read, Iosias begate Iakim, and Iakim begat Iechonias.
* 1.Chro. 3. 16,17.

18 ¶ Now the *birth of Iesus Christ was on this wise: when as his mother Mary was espoused to Ioseph (before they came together) shee was found with childe of the holy Ghost.

19 Then Ioseph her husband being a iust man, and not willing to make her a publique example, was minded to put her away priuily.

20 But while hee thought on these things, behold, the Angel of the Lord appeared vnto him in a dreame, saying, Ioseph thou sonne of Dauid, feare not to take vnto thee Mary thy wife: for that which is conceiued in her, is of the holy Ghost.

*Luke 1. 27.

21 And

16. Bible with Apocrypha

LONDON: ROBERT BARKER, 1611

2°: A⁶ B² C⁶ D⁴, A-5C⁶, A-Z⁶ 2A⁶; 732 ff. 357 x 225 mm. Black letter. Herbert 309

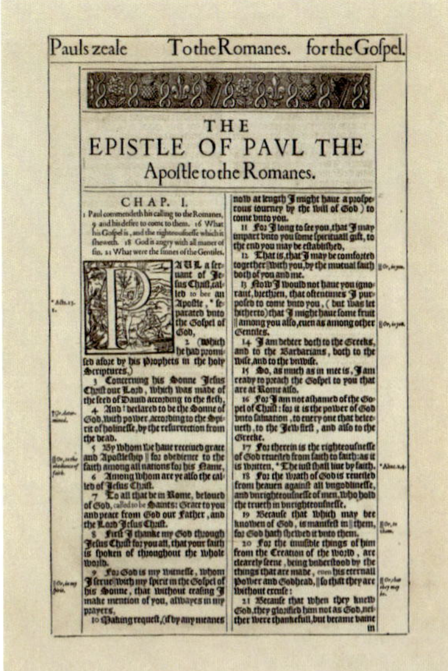

Fig. 16.1

Many folio Bibles bearing Barker's imprint and the date 1611 survive. Unlike editions of the text printed in 2011, they are not identical. Each of them has both a general title page and a secondary title page before the New Testament, but the information printed on these pages varies slightly from one group of copies to another. The date is either 1611 on both title pages or 1611 on one and 1613 on the other. The phrase *Appointed to be read in Churches* is missing from the New Testament title page in many copies and minor textual variations occur throughout the biblical text. One example is quoted time and again: the rendering of verse 3:15 in the Book of Ruth. Some copies read *and he went into the citie,* others read *and she went into the citie.* The best Hebrew manuscripts have the masculine form of the verb, the Vulgate has the feminine, and the context seems to require a feminine pronoun in English.[55]

55. Norton 2005: 57.

The Bible described here belongs to the group of copies that have the date 1611 and the phrase *Appointed to be read in Churches* on both title pages and the reading *and he went into the citie* in Ruth 3:15. It is considered the first edition of the King James Bible, its *editio princeps.*

The biblical text is printed in black letter within ruled borders, two columns to a page, 59 lines to a column. The chapter summaries, the marginal notes, and the occasional words added by the Translators and not found in the original texts are printed in roman type. A comparison between the printed text and its Hebrew and Greek ultimate sources reveals that many words added by the Translators are not printed in roman type. The lack of consistency may be due to the Translators, to the printers or to both groups. Later editions have strived to correct it.

The prefatory material of the first edition, running for 18 folios from A1 to D4, includes the dedication, the preface, the calendar and list of lessons, and a table of contents. Between this first section of the Bible and the beginning of Genesis, most editions printed between 1611 and November 1620 include a separate work consisting of the *Genealogies of Holy Scriptures* and a map of the Holy Land, both compiled by John Speed (*c.* 1552–1629), a well-known historian and cartographer. The *Genealogies* are signed A-C⁶ and paged 1-34 while the two folios of the map

have no identifying signature. Apparently the decision to attach this section
to the printed Bible was made by the Translators or the revisers. Samuel Ward,
a member of the Second Cambridge Company, mentions it at the very end
of his report to the Synod of Dort on 20 November 1618: "Lastly that a very
perfect Genealogy and map of the Holy Land should be joined to the work."[56]

The New Testament starts on a new sheet with a new register of signatures and could be bound and sold separately, if need be, but the Apocrypha
cannot be detached from the Old Testament. The general title page is a beautiful
engraving by the Flemish artist Cornelis Boel, who had been born in Antwerp
about the year 1580 and was living in Richmond at the time. Its upper part has
a representation of the Trinity consisting of the Tetragrammaton, the Dove of
the Holy Spirit, and the *Agnus Dei,* surrounded by the sun and the moon and
a group of Apostles. Andrew, the patron saint of Scotland, James' original
kingdom, is shown in a prominent place hugging his cross. On the three sides
of the engraved image, the artist represented the four Evangelists, Moses and
Aaron, and the pelican feeding her young with her blood, a medieval symbol
of Jesus' Passion (see Cat. 17). For the title page of the New Testament, Robert
Barker reused the large woodcut border that had embellished his 1602 edition
of the Bishops' Bible (see Cat. 13). There are no illustrations in the Bible, except
for those in the *Genealogies,* but there are many head pieces, vignettes, and
ornamental initials. As a rule, larger initials are used at the beginning of a book
and smaller ones at the beginning of a chapter, but there is no absolute consistency.
Initials representing Daphne being transformed into a laurel (see Fig 16.1) or Pan
playing his pipe may have been borrowed from a book on mythology. The large
initial at the beginning of Matthew's Gospel, shown here,
has the same origin. It includes an image of Neptune driving his chariot.[57] In
1568 Richard Jugge had decorated the Bishops' Bible with initials taken from an
edition of Ovid's *Metamorphoses.*

56. Pollard 1911: 339
(= 142 in facsimile edition)

57. Norton 2005: 51–53

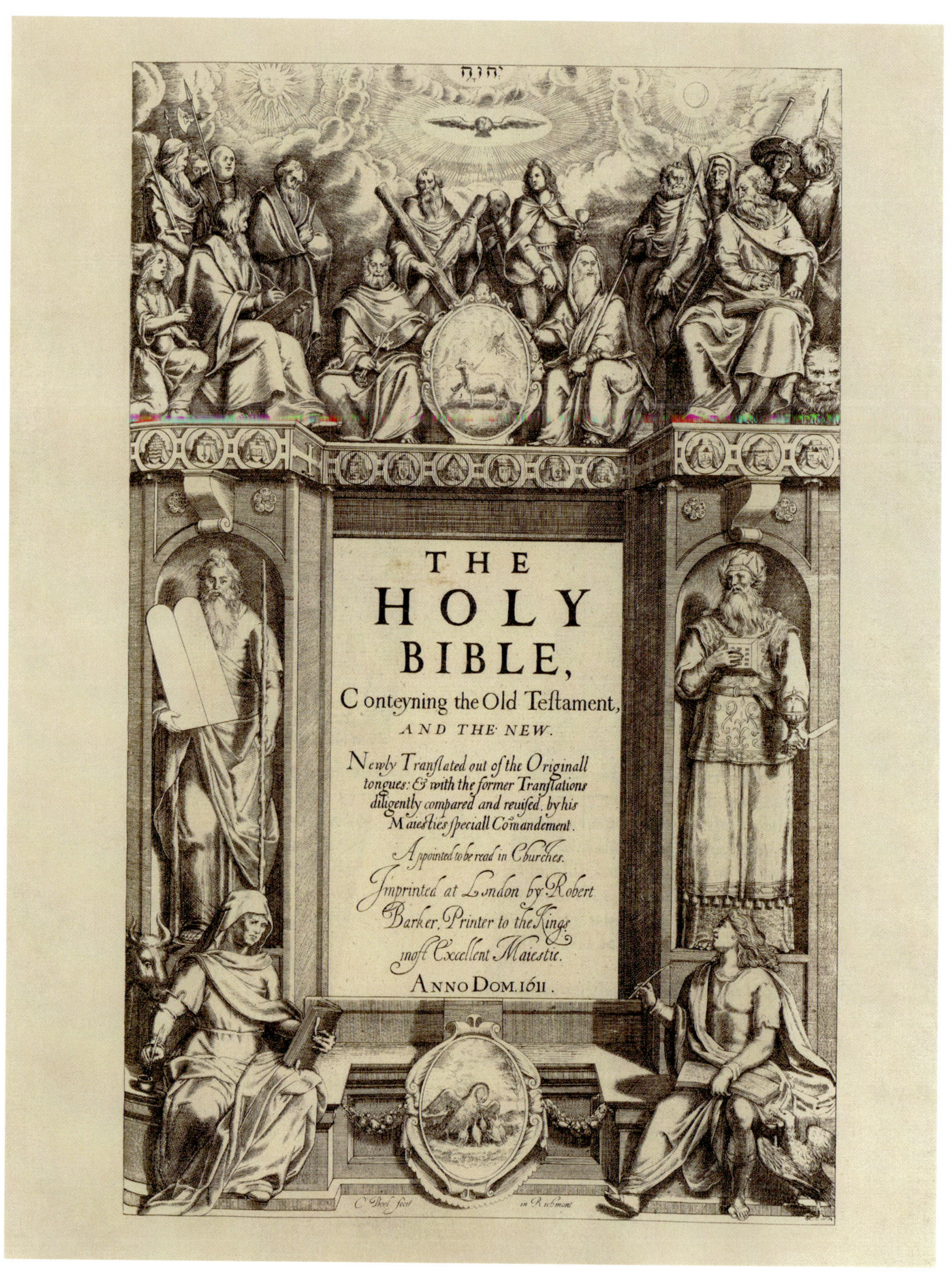

17. Bible with Apocrypha

17. Bible with Apocrypha |

2°: A⁶ B² C⁶ D⁴, A-5C⁶, A-Z⁶ 2A⁶; 732 ff. 357 x 225 mm. Black letter. Herbert 319

This is the second folio edition of the King James text, commonly known as the "Great She Bible," after its reading in Ruth 3:15: *and she went into the citie.* The copy described here, open to show the critical reading in Ruth 3:15, has the general title page engraved by Boel and the 1602 border in the New Testament title page. The date 1611 and the phrase *Appointed to be read in Churches* are printed on both title pages. In Matthew 26:36 the correct reading of the "He" Bible *Then cometh Jesus* was replaced with the erroneous *Then cometh Judas.* It appears that most sheets of the "She" Bible, if not all of them, were printed in 1611, but the edition was not released until 1613.

The two printings of 1611 did not provide enough copies to saturate the market for folio Bibles. Over the next few years Barker produced a folio in black letter in 1613, his first folio in roman type in 1616, and another folio in black letter in 1617.[58]

58. Herbert 322, 349, 353

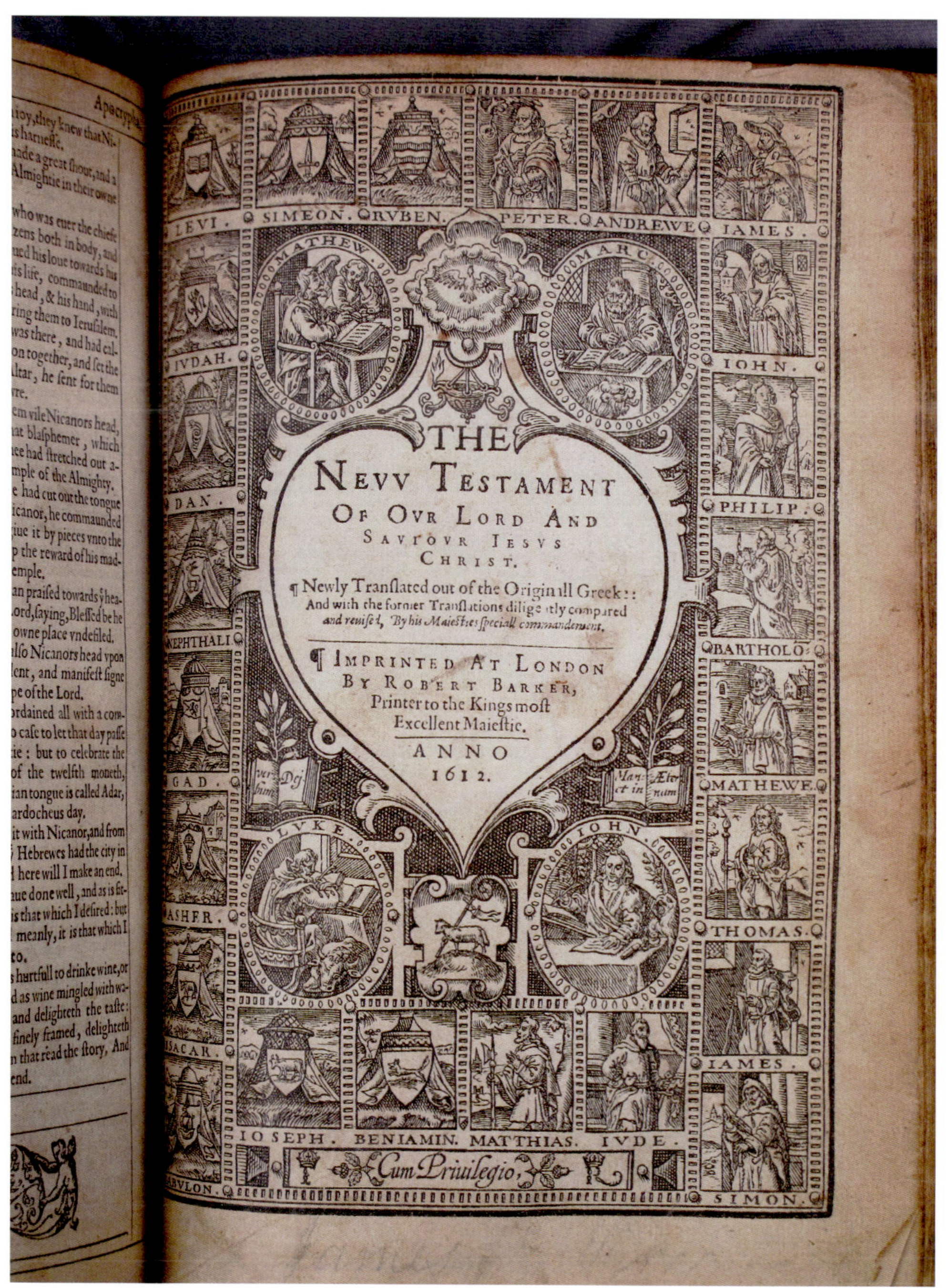

18. Bible with Apocrypha

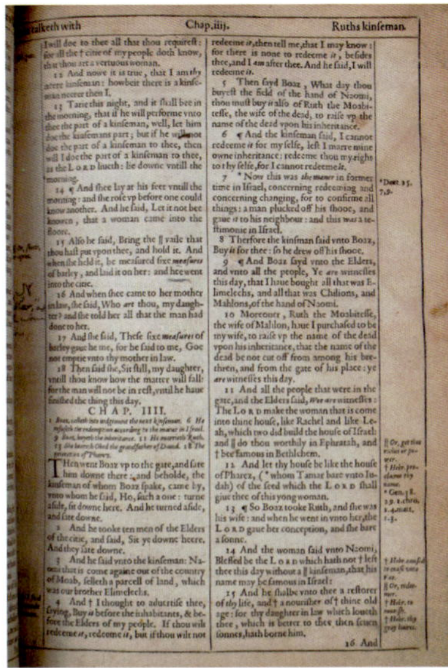

Fig. 18.1

The first edition of the King James text, published in 1611, embodied the prototype of a Bible *appointed to be read in churches.* For private use, more portable, and cheaper Bibles were printed within a year. In 1612, Barker produced both a quarto and an octavo edition of the King James text. Both are close reprints of the 1611 first edition, but look strikingly different: not only are they smaller and easier to handle, they are also printed in a different typeface. While the folio was printed in the traditional black letter, the pages of the two 1612 Bibles look much lighter and modern because they are printed in roman type.

The 1611 folio used roman type to create a strong visual difference between the biblical text and any editorial additions, such as chapter summaries, marginal notes, and words supplied by the Translators and not found in the Hebrew and Greek originals. To preserve this contrast, the 1612 quarto replaced the roman type of the first edition with italics. The practice was adopted in all the early editions of the King James Bible printed in roman type and is still used in contemporary scholarly editions. As the 1611 text was revised over the centuries, scholars continued to identify words supplied by the Translators and attempted to standardize the use of italics.

The general title page of the quarto is a reduction of the Boel engraving made by Jaspar Isaac (1585–1654), a Flemish artist who also worked in Paris. For the title page of the New Testament, shown here, Robert Barker recycled the engraving he was using at the time for his quarto editions of the Geneva Bible.[59] The title, which omits the reference to church reading, is printed in a heart-shaped space surrounded by a border that depicts the dove of the Holy Spirit, and the *Agnus Dei,* the 12 tribes of Israel, the 12 Apostles, and the four Evangelists. The phrase *Verbum Dei Manet in Aeternum* ("the word of God endures forever") is printed on two open books below the title. In Ruth 3:15 the 1612 quarto reads *he went into the citie* (Fig. 18.1) and so does the 1612 octavo displayed nearby. Both include the *Genealogies* and the map, reprinted page for page from the 1611 folio. Their New Testaments do not start on a new sheet of paper and cannot be detached from the Apocrypha.

59. Herbert 307 and 308

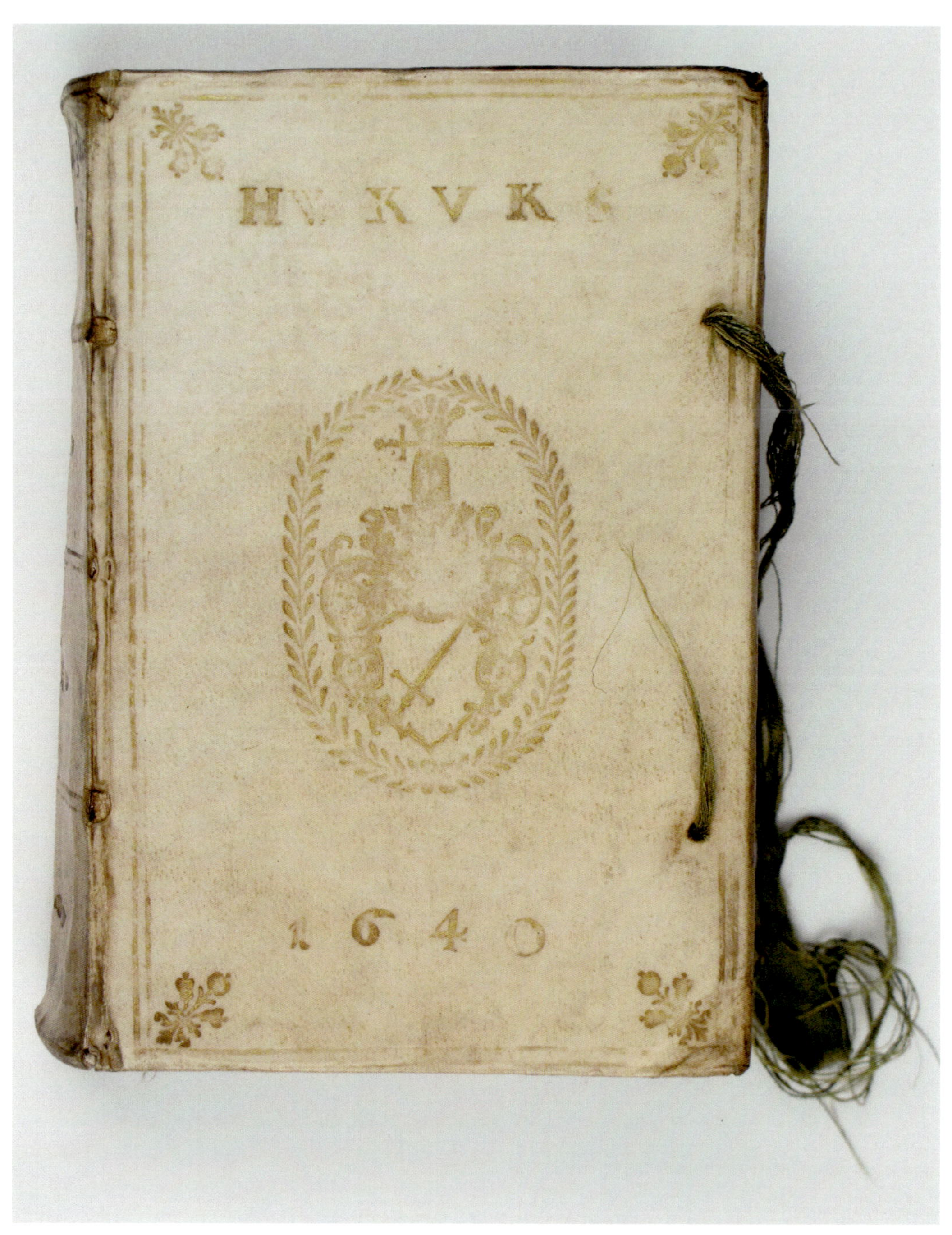

19. Bible with Apocrypha

LONDON: ROBERT BARKER, 1612

8°: A-3N⁸ 3O⁴; 476 ff. 157 x 99 mm. Herbert 315

This is the first pocket-size edition of the King James Bible and the first one
printed without Miles Smith's preface, *The Translators to the Reader*. Following
Barker's example, the preface was dropped from all octavo editions of the 1611
text ever published.

Textually, both the first quarto and the first octavo editions of the King
James Bible follow closely the 1611 folio. Some errors are common to the folio
and the octavo, but are corrected in the quarto. In Exodus 14:10, for instance the
phrase *the children of Israel lift up their eyes and behold, the Egyptians marched
after them and they were sore afraid* is printed twice in the folio and the octavo,
while in the quarto it appears, correctly, only once. Examples such as this one
led Scrivener to believe that the octavo is the earlier edition and the slightly more
correct quarto was printed later in 1612.[60] In the octavo edition, a funny misprint
appears in Psalm 119:161, where some copies read *Printers have persecuted me
without a cause* instead of *Princes*. The error was caught and corrected while the
sheet was being printed. The copy described here has the correct reading.

In the octavo edition both title pages have the heart-shaped design originally used for the Geneva Bible. A small engraving representing the Creation is
inserted before the beginning of Genesis.

This copy is displayed closed to show its vellum binding dated 1640 and
stamped with the initials and shield of Johann (Hans) Wilhelm Kress von
Kressenstein. Fragments of the green silk ties that once kept the volume closed
are still attached to its covers. Towards the middle of the seventeenth century,
Kress had quite a reputation as a connoisseur and his bookplates are found on
books and manuscripts scattered through many European libraries. Engraved
portraits of four other members of the Kress family are bound in front of the Bible.

60. Scrivener 1884: 15

THE NEW TESTAMENT OF OUR LORD AND SAVIOUR JESUS CHRIST.

Newly tranſlated out of the original Greek : and with the former tranſlatoins diligently compared and reviſed by his majeſties ſpeciall command.

¶ Appointed to be read in churches.

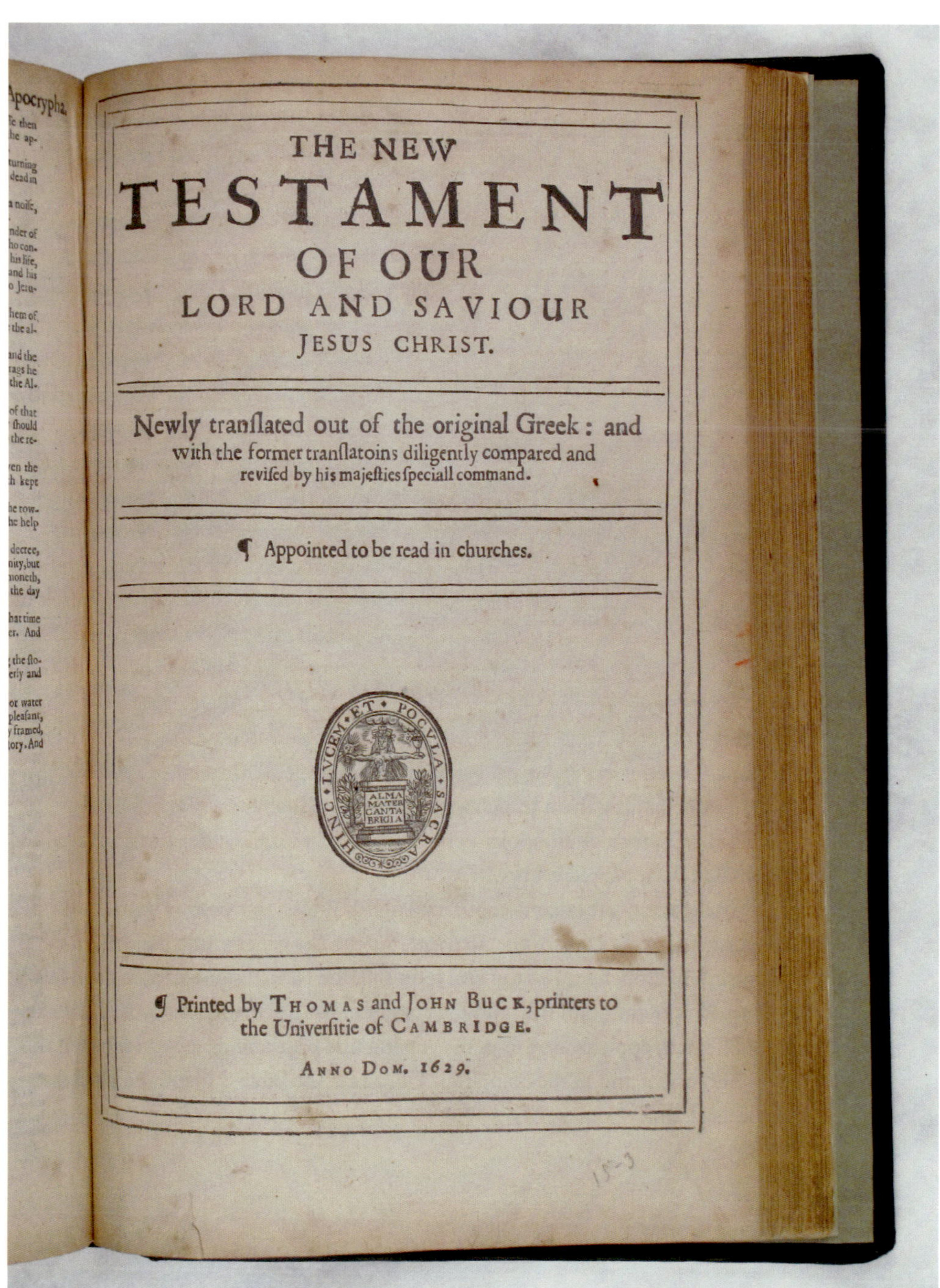

¶ Printed by THOMAS and JOHN BUCK, printers to the Univerſitie of CAMBRIDGE.

ANNO DOM. 1629.

21. Bible with Apocrypha

CAMBRIDGE: THOMAS BUCK AND JOHN BUCK, PRINTERS TO THE
UNIVERSITY, 1629

2°: ¶⁶ A-3I⁶ 3K⁴ 3L-4A⁶ 4B⁴; 430 ff. (including 2 blanks). 256 x 167 mm. Herbert 424

The Bibles published by Robert Barker and his associates were essentially reprints
of the 1611 text with occasional corrections of existing misprints and inadvertent
additions of new typographical errors. In 1629 the University of Cambridge published the first revised edition of the Translators' work. A group of Cambridge
dons read it against the Hebrew and Greek originals and proceeded to make
it more literal and more scholarly.[61] The changes they made may not have any
significant impact on the meaning of the English version, but they certainly raised
its level of accuracy. The revisers replaced singulars with plurals and plurals with
singulars, and substituted possessive pronouns for definite articles in order to
bring the translation closer to the original texts. The Jacobean Translators had been
instructed to use the common English forms of the personal or geographical names
in the original texts.[62] The Cambridge editors strived to bring more consistency in
this area and unified the spelling of many names whose form fluctuates in the 1611
edition. According to Norton[63] their revision resulted in 221 new readings and 178
new spellings in addition to confirming 59 variant readings and 34 variant spelling.
91% of the changes they made were accepted into what became the standard text.
The editors of the 1629 Bible also corrected the marginal notes and the use of italics
for words not found in the original texts.

Thomas Buck (*c.* 1593–1670) and his younger brother John Buck (*c.*
1597–1680) were appointed printers to the University of Cambridge in 1625. The
beautiful Bible they produced in 1629 is printed in roman type according to an
updated system of spelling. The 1611 edition used the traditional spelling with no
j and with *v* at the beginning of a word and *u* in its middle. The spelling of the
1629 Cambridge edition is quite modern. Words that had been printed as *vp, vs*
and *ouer* or *iaw, iealous,* and *ioyne* in 1611 are spelled *up, us* and *over* or *jaw,*
jealous, and *join* in the Cambridge edition.

According to a pamphlet published in 1641, the first 1629 Cambridge Bible
sold for 10 shillings unbound.[64] B.J. McMullin[65] examined 39 copies of the 1629
edition and determined that they were printed on seven different qualities of
paper. We may assume that the prices varied with the paper. The general title page,
lacking from the copy described here, was engraved by John Payne (1607–1647)
and represents Moses and David, the four Evangelists, the Last Supper, and a hart
drinking from a brook, an allusion to Psalm 42:1 *As the hart panteth after the water*
brooks, so panteth my soul after thee, O God.

The Bible is open to show the title page of the New Testament.

61. See Norton 2005: 82-89

62. See page 56

63. 2005: 82-89

64. Herbert, p. 182–184

65. 1984: 383 and passim

THE NEW TESTAMENT OF OUR LORD AND SAVIOUR JESUS CHRIST,

Nevvly tranſlated out of the originall Greek, and with the former tranſlations diligently compared and reviſed, by his Majeſties ſpeciall command.

¶ Appointed to be read in churches.

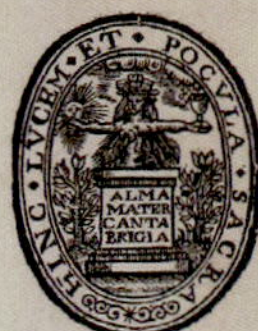

Printed by THOMAS BUCK and ROGER DANIEL, printers to the Univerſitie of Cambridge. Anno Dom. 1638.

22. Bible with Apocrypha

CAMBRIDGE: THOMAS BUCK AND ROGER DANIEL, PRINTERS TO THE
UNIVERSITY, 1638

2°: A-3G⁶ 3H-3I⁴, 3K-3X⁶ 3Y⁴, A-R⁶; 506 ff. (including 2 blanks). 329 x 205 mm. Herbert 520

At Cambridge, the process of revising the King James Bible did not stop with the
publication of the 1629 folio. A second revised edition was issued in 1638 and
remained the standard text of the King James Bible until 1762. It was the work of
four scholars: Samuel Ward (d. 1643), Thomas Goad (1576–1638), John Bois, and
Joseph Mede (1586–1639). Ward and Bois had been members of the original team
of Translators. Both had worked on the Second Cambridge Company in charge
of the Apocrypha, and Bois had also represented the Company when the final
revision was made (see Ill. 5). The 1638 edition completed and corrected the work
done one decade earlier and brought increased accuracy and consistency to the
King James Bible. It contributed to the standard text 121 readings and 114 spellings
of proper names.[66]

66. Norton 2005: 89-91.

The two printers, Thomas Buck, who had also worked on the 1629 edition,
and Roger Daniel (active 1627–1666), were so proud of their work that they
promised a free copy of the 1638 folio to any person who could discover an error.
In the late nineteenth century, Scrivener[67] did find five misprints, including the
one in Acts 6:3, where the incorrect reading *whom ye may appoint* had replaced
the traditional reading *whom we may appoint*. The error suggests that the Apostles
wanted the faithful to appoint their own deacons. For a long time it was considered
a deliberate distortion of the Greek text and the responsibility for the reading was
falsely assigned to Oliver Cromwell and the Puritans. Strangely enough, the same
misprint occurs in a duodecimo Bible printed by Isaiah Thomas in 1797.[68]

67. 1884: 23 and 4.
For Scrivener see Cat. 48

68. Hills 57

The copy described here, which lacks the general title page, is bound with
a defective copy of the *Book of Common Prayer* and an edition of the *Metrical
Psalms* published by Buck and Daniel in 1638. It is open to show the title page of
the New Testament.

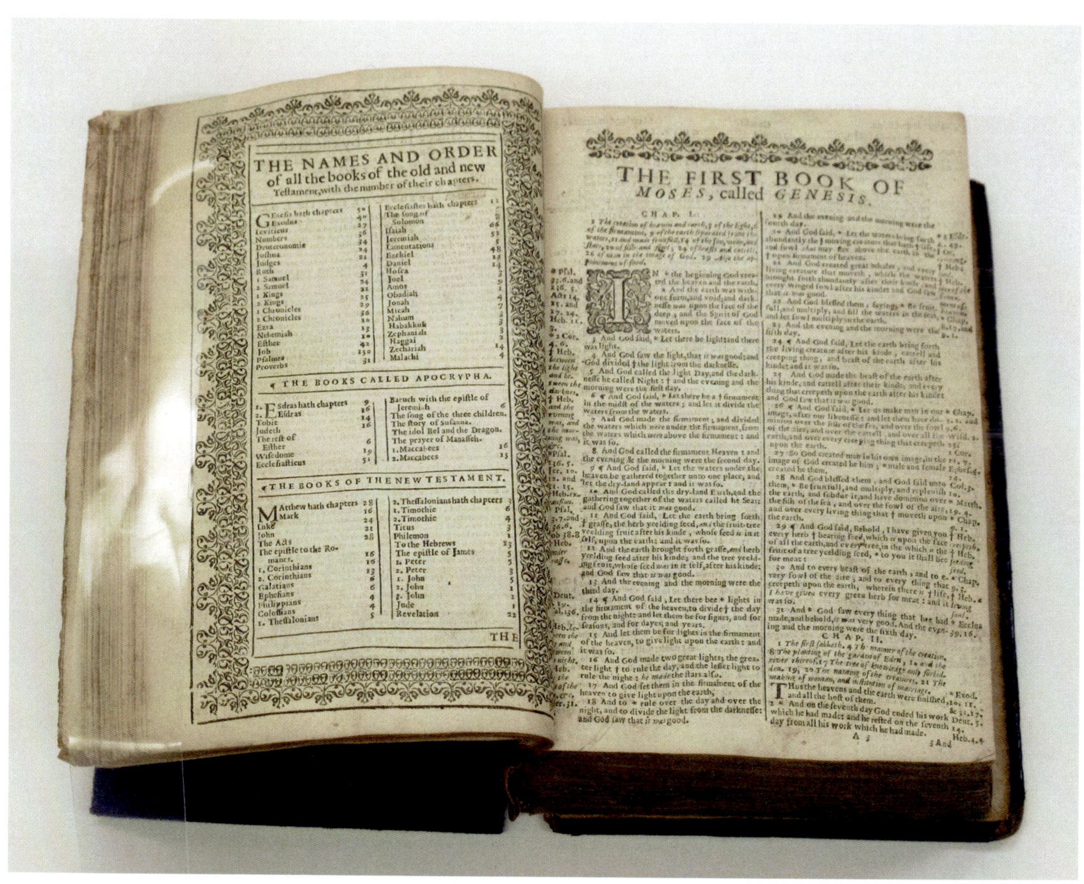

23. Bible with Apocrypha

Edinburgh: [Robert Young], 1633

8°: A-2X⁸ 2Y⁴ 3A-3L⁸ 3M⁴; 450 ff. 156 x 98 mm. Herbert 476

The first Bible printed in Scotland was a folio edition of the Geneva version issued by Thomas Bassandyne and Alexander Arbuthnot in 1579. Two small-size editions of the New Testament in the same version were printed in the Netherlands in 1601 and 1603 and distributed in Scotland, and a second folio of the Geneva text was issued in Edinburgh in 1610. The third complete Bible printed in Scotland was the octavo edition of the King James text issued in Edinburgh in 1633, probably to celebrate the coronation of Charles I in Edinburgh in the month of June. The Bible was produced by Robert Young (active 1625–43), who had worked in London since 1625 and was appointed King's Printer for Scotland in April 1532.

A set of 76 plates based on engravings made by the Flemish artist Boetius à Bolswert *(c.* 1585–1633) was added to the text of the New Testament in many copies of the 1633 Bible, but not in the one on display. These engravings had been first published in Antwerp, in 1623, as part of a small devotional book on the life and passion of Jesus Christ written by the Jesuit Jean Bourgeois. The London print dealer Robert Peake (active 1635–d. 1667) made a fortune by selling the Bourgeois engravings to book dealers who inserted them in Robert Young's Bibles.[69] The illustrated Bibles outraged the Scottish Protestants, who perceived the engravings as evidence of idolatry and found particularly offensive a depiction of the Assumption of the Virgin inserted before the title page of the New Testament.

In the copy described here the biblical text is preceded by an edition of the *Book of Common Prayer* of the Church of England printed by Robert Young in 1634. Three years later, when Charles I tried to replace the Scottish Prayer Book with the Anglican one in the liturgy, there was a riot in the principal church in Edinburgh and the congregation "threw their clasped Bibles and the very stools they sat on, at the minister's head."[70] Robert Young returned to London in 1638, but was reappointed King's Printer for Scotland three years later. In this exhibition his Bible is open at the beginning of Genesis.

69. De Hamel 2001: 249–251

70. Dobson 1887: 173

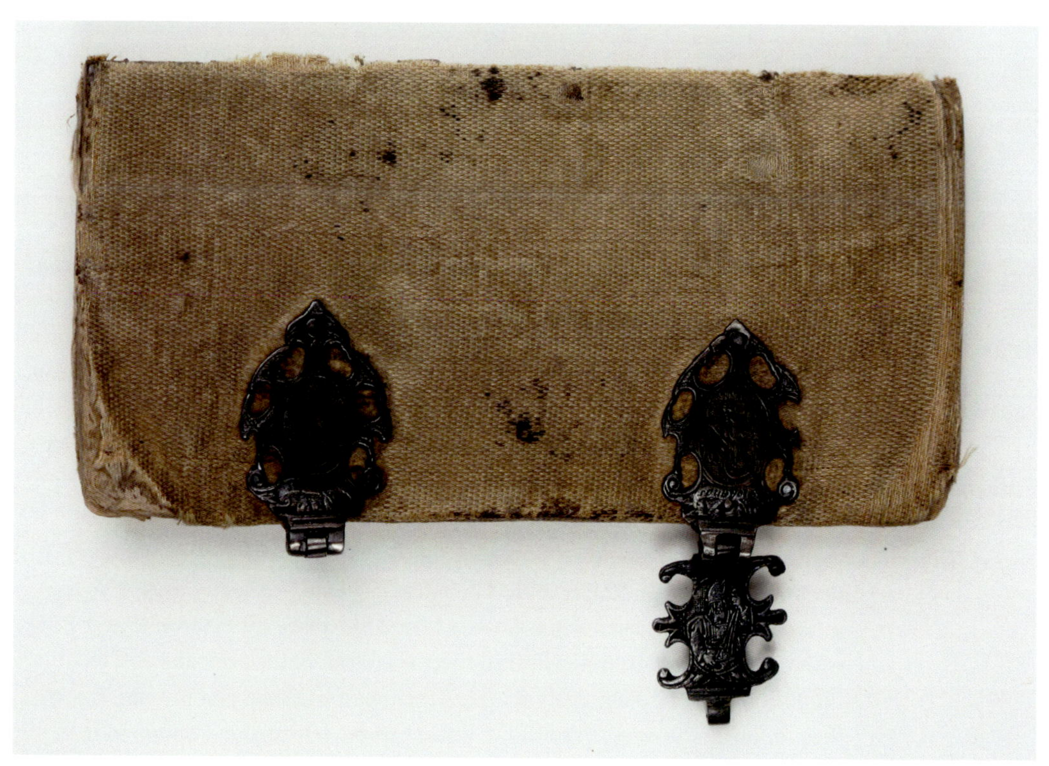

24. New Testament

A twentyfourmo is a book in which the sheet is folded into 24 leaves.

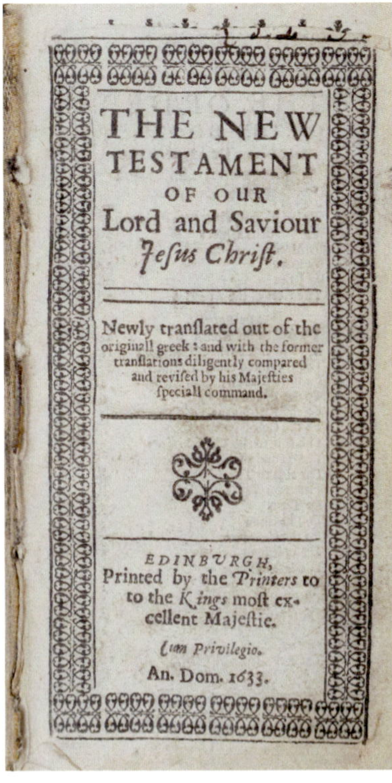

Fig. 24.1

Miniature editions of the New Testament in English are rare and their survival rate is extremely low. Herbert's standard bibliography of English Scriptures lists only six editions printed before 1633 in the format known as twentyfourmo. Robert Young, the King's Printer for Scotland, issued the seventh one. He printed it in single column, without marginal notes. This copy is bound with an edition of the *Metrical Psalms* published by the Stationers' Company in London, in 1635. It has a beautiful contemporary binding of rose velvet, now faded and napless, with silver clasps, now tarnished. Its edges are tooled and gilt. While the Bible is displayed closed Fig. 24.1 shows its title page.

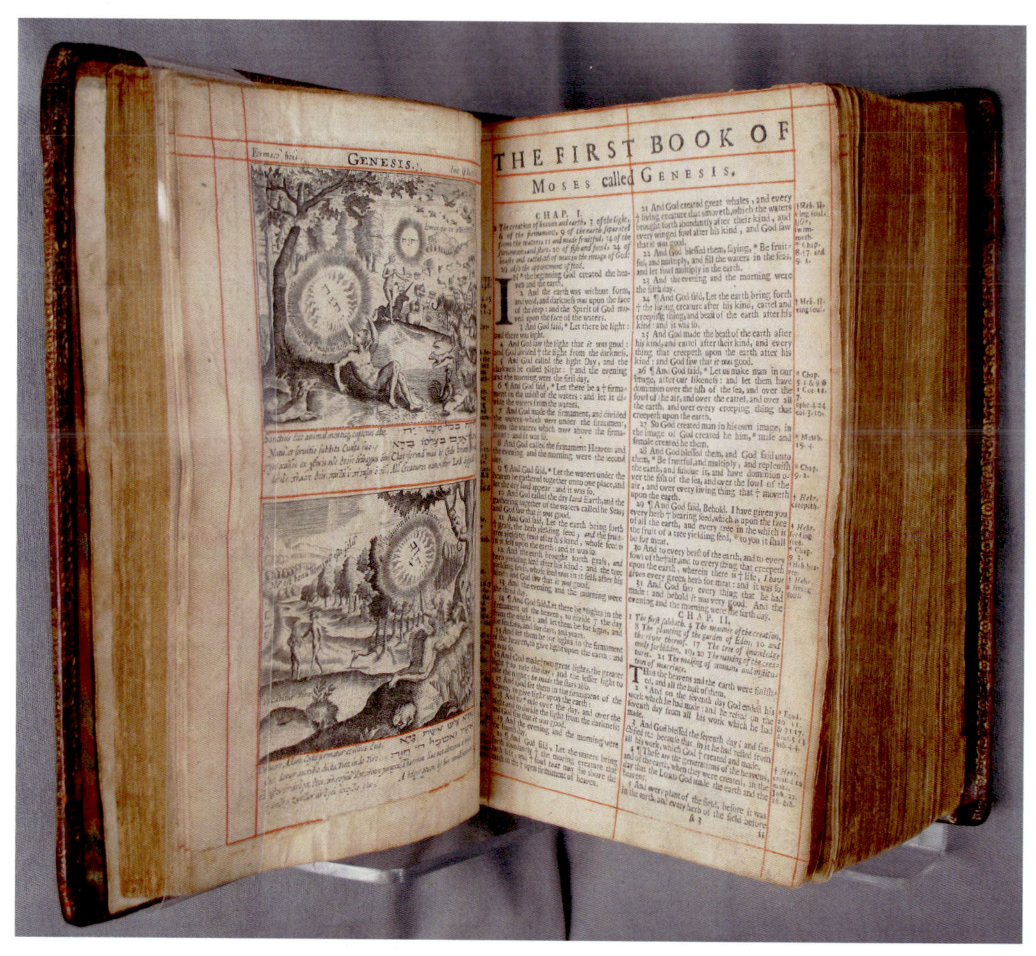

25. Bible with Apocrypha

71. Herbert 546

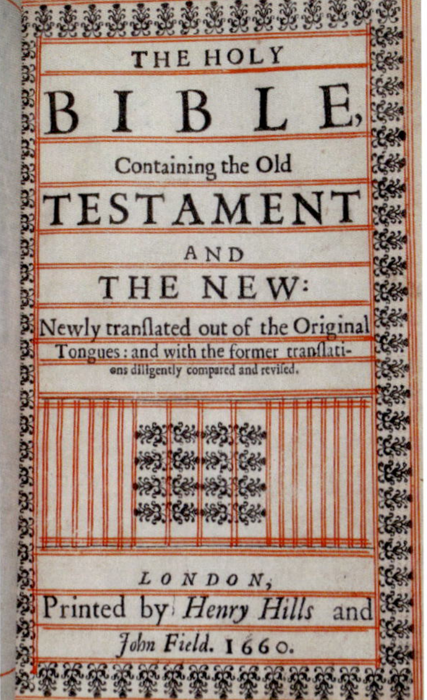

Fig. 25.1

This volume is remarkable for the 183 engraved plates added to the text after its publication. Many of them are also found in another octavo Bible printed in London in 1640 by Robert Barker and the *Assigns of John Bill* that belongs in the Rare Bible Collection @ MOBIA.[71] In both Bibles, the Old Testament is embellished with smaller engravings, printed two to a page, while the New Testament has much larger single-page images. In the 1660 Bible, the first 28 engravings, depicting scenes from the beginning of Genesis, from the Creation to Noah's Ark, have captions printed in Hebrew, Greek, and Latin. Starting with the end of the Noah story all the captions are printed in English. The original engravings were probably created on the Continent, maybe in the Netherlands.

Those added to the New Testament were copied from a Catholic publication, like the images inserted in the Bibles printed in Scotland in 1633 (see above Cat. 23). There is no reference to Catholic doctrine or practice in the 1660 copy, but the 1640 Bible includes a depiction of the Virgin and the Fifteen Mysteries of the Rosary that is unmistakably Catholic.

The 1660 Bible has a beautiful binding of red morocco in the "Cottage Roof" style. Its edges are gilt and its text ruled in red. The volume opens with a *Book of Common Prayer* published in 1665, and ends with a 1663 edition of the *Metrical Psalms*. Its printers, Henry Hills (active 1641–1688) and his partner John Field (active 1644–1668), leased from Oxford University the right to publish the King James Bible for a period of four years and paid the University 80 pounds per year.

The Bible is open to show the beginning of Genesis with its two inserted illustrations. Fig 25.1 is a photograph of its title page.

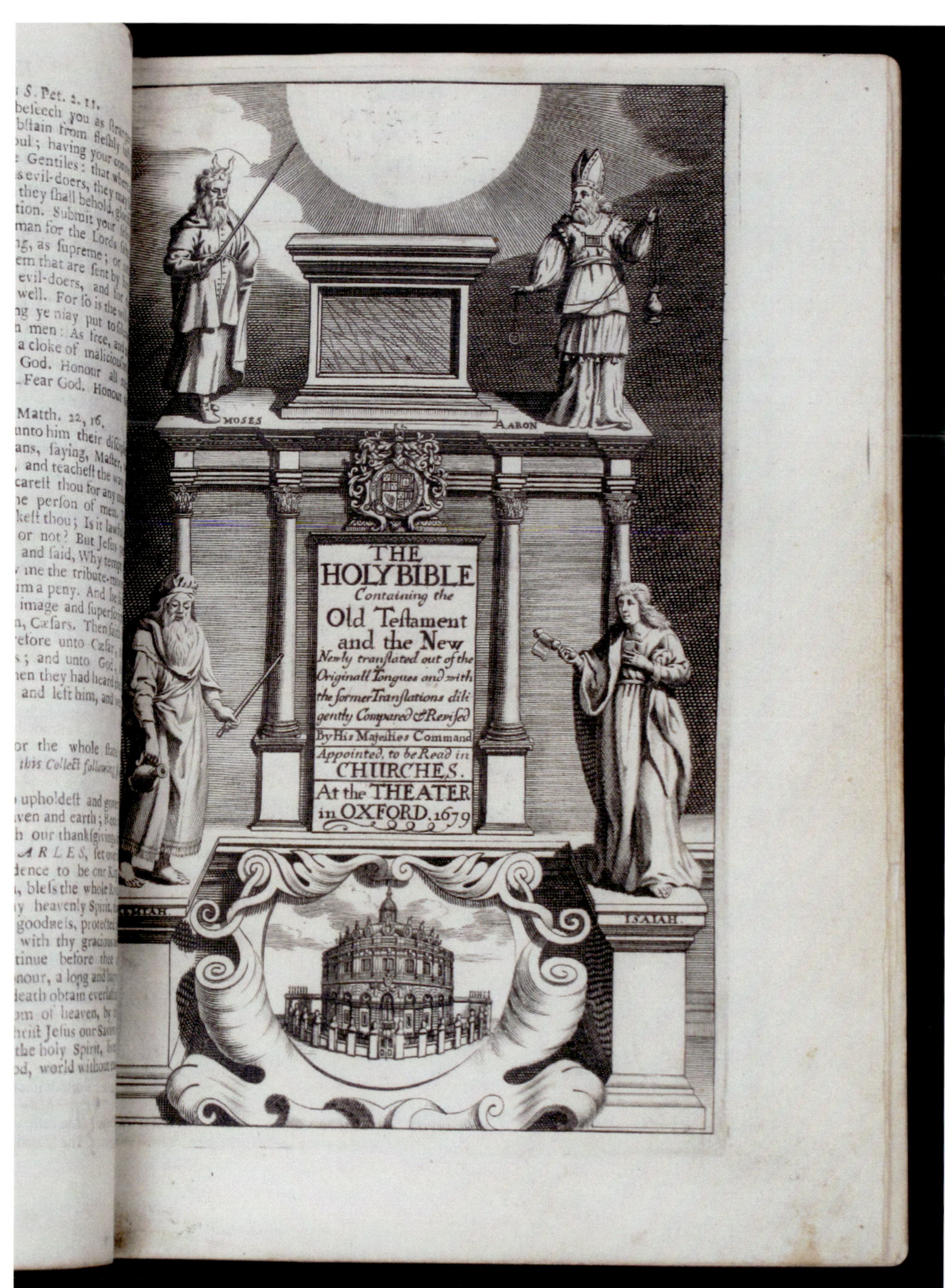

26. Bible with Apocrypha

OXFORD: AT THE THEATER, 1679

4°: A-2Z⁸ 3A⁸ 3B⁴ 3C², A-K⁸, A-P⁸; 556 ff. 176 x 125 mm. Herbert 744

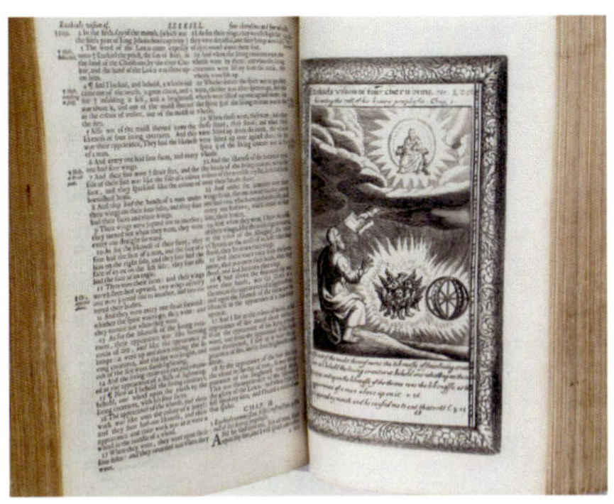

Fig. 26.1

Archbishop William Laud (1573–1645), Chancellor of the University of Oxford between 1630 and 1641, obtained in 1636 from Charles I a charter allowing the University to print "all manner of books" and an additional "privilege" to publish the King James Bible. The University entered into various agreements with the Stationers' Company of London and other printers and received money in exchange for not exercising its right to print Bibles. Its first edition of the King James text, released in 1675, was a relatively modest quarto. Its second edition, described here, appears to be the first English Bible with chronological information added to the marginal notes. The biblical chronology was taken from a treatise compiled by the Archbishop of Armagh, James Ussher (1581–1656), and first published in 1650–1654. At the time, many scholars, including Isaac Newton and Johannes Kepler, believed that the world was created around the year 4000 BC and assumed it would end 6000 years later, in AD 2000. If Peter was right when he wrote in his Second Epistle (3:8), "with the Lord, one day is like a thousand years," 6000 years did correspond to the six days of Creation. Ussher further refined this chronology and determined that Creation started at sunset on the day preceding Sunday, October 23, 4004 BC. In the 1679 Oxford Bible, the dates are given from the Year of Creation (*Anno Mundi*), not from the Year of the Lord (*Anno Domini*): the vision of Ezekiel, for instance, dates from 3509 and the birth of Jesus from 4000.

The Bible is open to show its engraved title page, which mentions and also depicts the Sheldonian Theatre. The building had been designed by Sir Christopher Wren and was completed in 1668. Its cellars were used as the University's printing shop.

This copy lacks the Apocrypha, signed A-K⁸ in other copies, and includes a large number of engraved plates added at an unknown date. In the Old Testament they are framed by an ornamental border and numbered from 1 to 80. In the New Testament they have no border and their numbers run from 2 to 110. Fig. 26.1 illustrates the opening that includes the first chapter of Ezekiel and a representation of the four cherubim and four wheels described in the prophet's vision. The date attributed to the event is 3509.

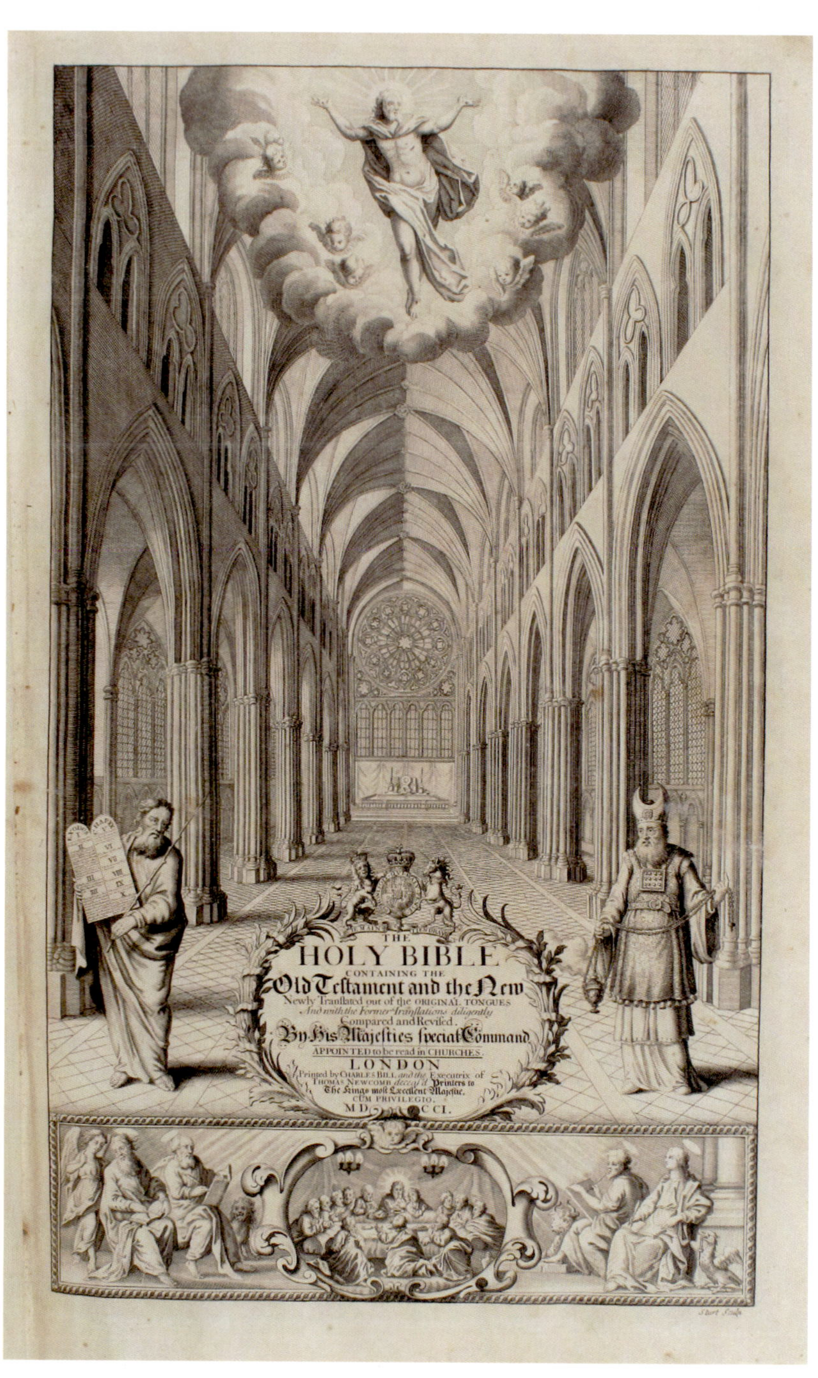

27. Bible with Apocrypha

This impressive folio, larger than any Bible previously published in England, marks the first attempt to provide a study edition of the King James text. After the end of Revelation it includes two densely printed tables that describe the subject matter of the two Testaments in chronological order and explain the system of weights, measures, and coins used in the biblical world. The second table was compiled by Richard Cumberland (1631–1718), Bishop of Peterborough. The chronology is attributed to William Lloyd (1627–1717), Bishop of Winchester. All dates are given in relation to the Nativity: Creation is dated to the year 4004 "before the Common Year of Christ" and the birth of Jesus to "the fifth year before the Common Account called Anno Domini."

The Bible was beautifully printed in the shop belonging to Ruth Newcombe (active 1643– 1701), the widow of Thomas Newcombe, and to her silent partner Charles Bill (active 1687–1701). The Bible is not illustrated, but the printers commissioned a set of woodcut initials carefully chosen to represent appropriate biblical scenes: Adam and Eve in the Garden of Eden at the beginning of Genesis, the conversion of Paul in the Pauline Epistles, the Way of the Cross in Luke's Gospel, etc. The engraved title page, shown here, depicts the interior of a Gothic cathedral with the resurrected Jesus ascending to heaven in the upper register, Moses and Aaron on each side of the title, and the four Evangelists and the Last Supper at the bottom of the page. The coat of arms of William III, King of England from 1689 to 1702, is inserted right above the title.

The editor of the 1769 Oxford text (see Cat. 31) made extensive use of a 1701 folio he described as "Bishop Lloyd's Bible." It is impossible to determine whether he meant the London folio displayed here or a slightly smaller one printed the same year at Oxford.[72]

72. Herbert 867

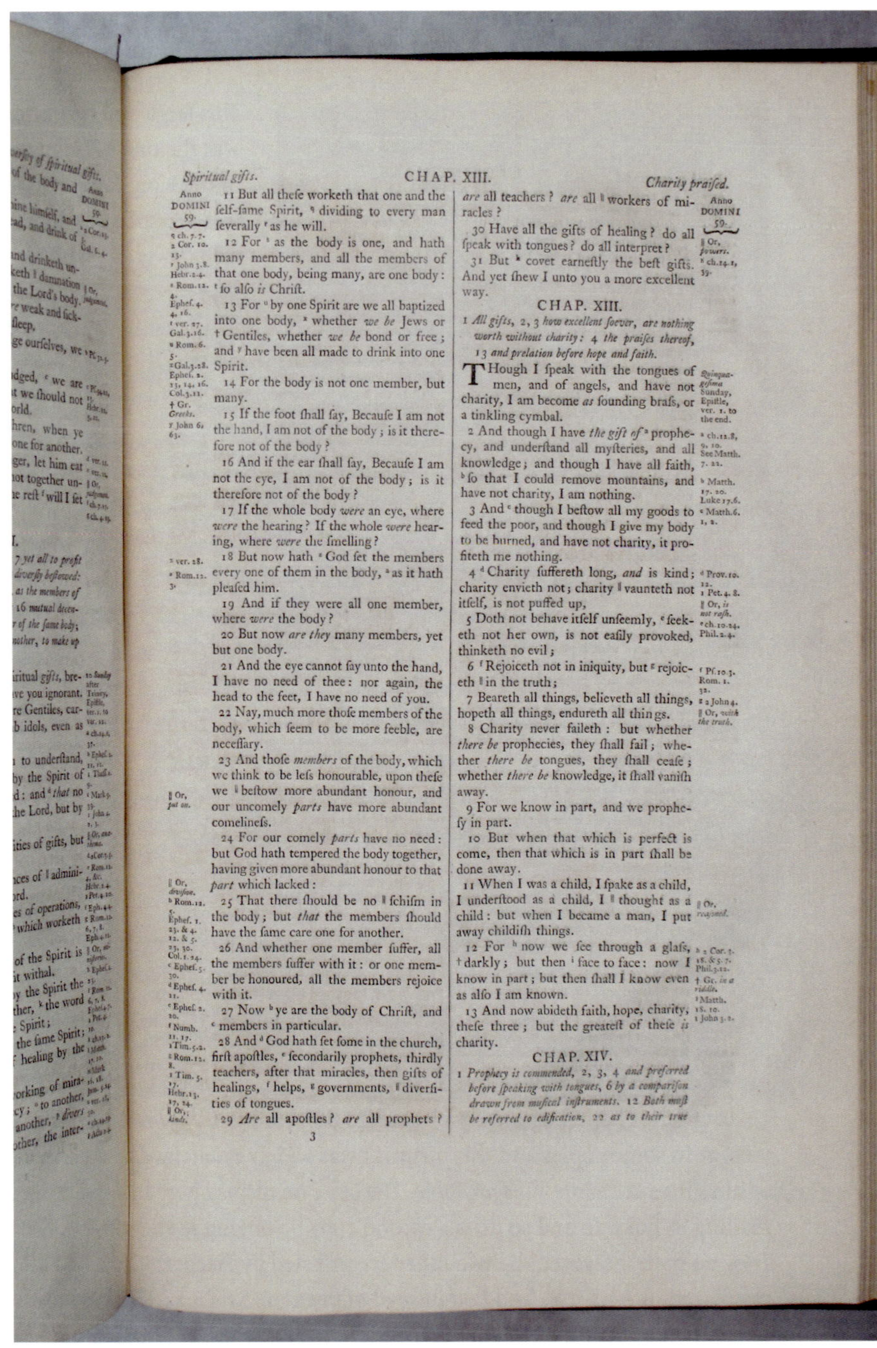

Anno DOMINI 59.

11 But all these worketh that one and the self-same Spirit, dividing to every man severally as he will.

12 For as the body is one, and hath many members, and all the members of that one body, being many, are one body: so also is Christ.

13 For by one Spirit are we all baptized into one body, whether *we be* Jews or † Gentiles, whether *we be* bond or free; and have been all made to drink into one Spirit.

14 For the body is not one member, but many.

15 If the foot shall say, Because I am not the hand, I am not of the body; is it therefore not of the body?

16 And if the ear shall say, Because I am not the eye, I am not of the body; is it therefore not of the body?

17 If the whole body *were* an eye, where *were* the hearing? If the whole *were* hearing, where *were* the smelling?

18 But now hath God set the members every one of them in the body, as it hath pleased him.

19 And if they were all one member, where *were* the body?

20 But now *are they* many members, yet but one body.

21 And the eye cannot say unto the hand, I have no need of thee: nor again, the head to the feet, I have no need of you.

22 Nay, much more those members of the body, which seem to be more feeble, are necessary.

23 And those *members* of the body, which we think to be less honourable, upon these we bestow more abundant honour, and our uncomely *parts* have more abundant comeliness.

24 For our comely *parts* have no need: but God hath tempered the body together, having given more abundant honour to that *part* which lacked:

25 That there should be no schism in the body; but *that* the members should have the same care one for another.

26 And whether one member suffer, all the members suffer with it: or one member be honoured, all the members rejoice with it.

27 Now ye are the body of Christ, and members in particular.

28 And God hath set some in the church, first apostles, secondarily prophets, thirdly teachers, after that miracles, then gifts of healings, helps, governments, diversities of tongues.

29 *Are* all apostles? *are* all prophets? *are* all teachers? *are* all workers of miracles?

30 Have all the gifts of healing? do all speak with tongues? do all interpret?

31 But covet earnestly the best gifts. And yet shew I unto you a more excellent way.

CHAP. XIII.

1 *All gifts,* 2, 3 *how excellent soever, are nothing worth without charity:* 4 *the praises thereof,* 13 *and prelation before hope and faith.*

THough I speak with the tongues of men, and of angels, and have not charity, I am become *as* sounding brass, or a tinkling cymbal.

2 And though I have *the gift of* prophecy, and understand all mysteries, and all knowledge; and though I have all faith, so that I could remove mountains, and have not charity, I am nothing.

3 And though I bestow all my goods to feed the poor, and though I give my body to be burned, and have not charity, it profiteth me nothing.

4 Charity suffereth long, *and* is kind; charity envieth not; charity vaunteth not itself, is not puffed up,

5 Doth not behave itself unseemly, seeketh not her own, is not easily provoked, thinketh no evil;

6 Rejoiceth not in iniquity, but rejoiceth in the truth;

7 Beareth all things, believeth all things, hopeth all things, endureth all things.

8 Charity never faileth: but whether *there be* prophecies, they shall fail; whether *there be* tongues, they shall cease; whether *there be* knowledge, it shall vanish away.

9 For we know in part, and we prophesy in part.

10 But when that which is perfect is come, then that which is in part shall be done away.

11 When I was a child, I spake as a child, I understood as a child, I thought as a child: but when I became a man, I put away childish things.

12 For now we see through a glass, † darkly; but then face to face: now I know in part; but then shall I know even as also I am known.

13 And now abideth faith, hope, charity, these three; but the greatest of these *is* charity.

CHAP. XIV.

1 *Prophecy is commended,* 2, 3, 4 *and preferred before speaking with tongues,* 6 *by a comparison drawn from musical instruments.* 12 *Both must be referred to edification,* 22 *as to their true*

3

29. Bible with Apocrypha

CAMBRIDGE: JOSEPH BENTHAM, 1762

2°: A-2O⁸, 2P-3D⁸ 3E², ₌A-₌M⁸, 3F-3X⁸ 3Z⁴; 620 ff. 298 x 190 mm. Herbert 1142

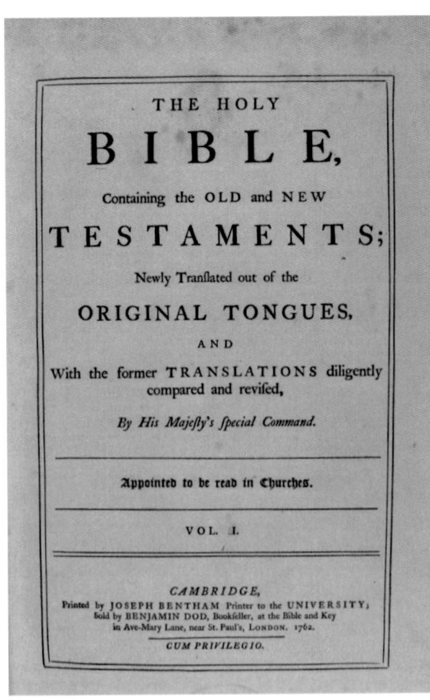

Fig. 29.1

The University of Cambridge resumed its efforts to produce a scholarly text of the King James Bible soon after the publication of the 1638 folio described earlier (see Cat. 22). Francis Sawyer Parris (1707–1760), Master of Sydney Sussex College since 1746 and University Librarian, spent the last decades of his distinguished academic career preparing a new folio edition of the 1611 text. He had already overseen the printing of a small duodecimo Bible in 1743. The 1762 folio, published two years after his death, contributed significantly to the creation of a standard text of the King James Bible. Like his predecessors, Parris tried to bring the translation closer to the original texts by checking the textual variants, using the appropriate grammatical number, changing the word order, etc. He also tried to improve the spelling. Parris gave its modern form to a well-known verse from Paul's First Epistle to the Corinthians (13:2): *though I have all faith … and have not charity, I am nothing.* In the 1611 edition the text read: *and have no charity.*

Both the 1762 folio and its quarto companion were seen through the press by H. Therold, a Fellow of Magdalene College. The decision to add a reprint of the Chronological Table first issued in the 1701 London folio (see Cat. 27) may have been taken by Therold. The two 1762 Cambridge Bibles lack Smith's original preface *The Translators to the Reader* in the copies belonging to the Rare Bible Collection @ MOBIA. If this is not an accident, the University of Cambridge was the first scholarly publisher to drop this important text from its King James Bibles. The copy on display is open to show the beginning of 1 Corinthians 13. Fig. 29.1 is a photograph of its title page.

THE

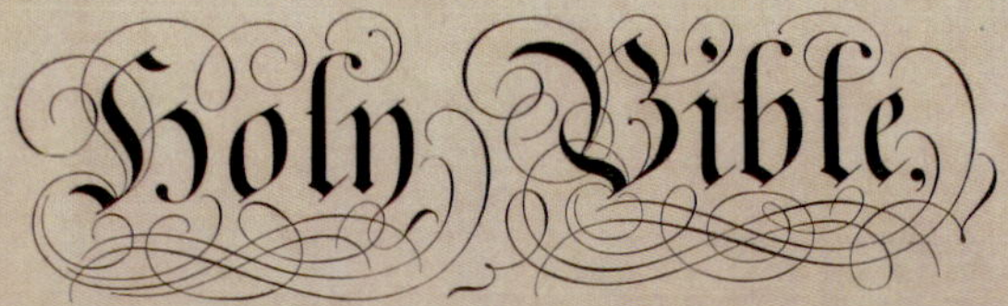

Holy Bible,

CONTAINING THE

OLD TESTAMENT

AND

THE NEW:

Tranflated out of the

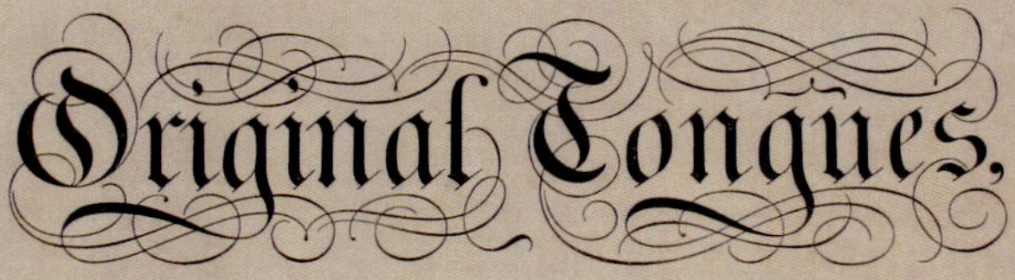

Original Tongues,

AND

With the former TRANSLATIONS

Diligently Compared and Revifed,

By His MAJESTY's Special Command.

<hr>

APPOINTED TO BE READ IN CHURCHES.

<hr>

CAMBRIDGE,

Printed by *JOHN BASKERVILLE*, Printer to the UNIVERSITY.

M DCC LXIII.

CUM PRIVILEGIO.

30. Bible with Apocrypha

CAMBRIDGE: JOHN BASKERVILLE, 1763

2°: A-13D² 13E¹, a-e² f¹; 573 ff. 415 x 240 mm. Herbert 1146

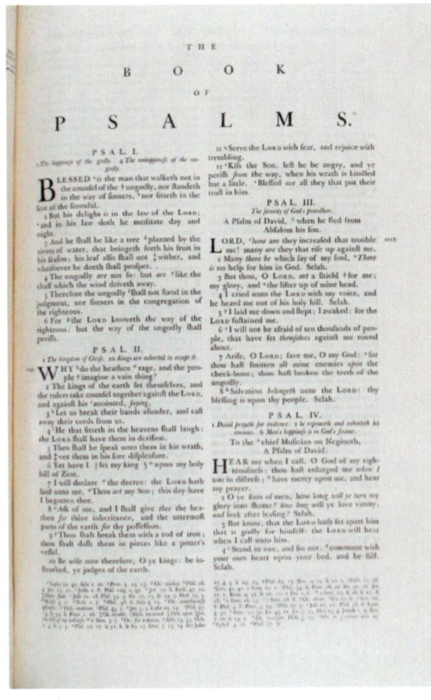

Fig. 30.1

This magnificent Bible, one of the most beautiful books ever printed, is the masterpiece of John Baskerville (1706–1775), who had been printer to the University of Cambridge since 1758. Throughout his career Baskerville strove to achieve a perfect balance between type, layout, paper, and ink. He used to discard a quarter of the sheets he printed and was not satisfied until he obtained pages of even color and inking. Not surprisingly, his 1763 Bible cost twice as much as any contemporary folio Bible. Although forgotten after his death, Baskerville's work was rediscovered a few decades later. The 50 or so books he had produced began to be actively collected and his original punches eventually found their way into the Cambridge University Library. Many of the fonts released by type foundries such as Linotype and Monotype are revivals of Baskerville's typefaces and bear his name. Sir Arthur Conan Doyle paid Baskerville an indirect homage in 1901, when he used his family name in one of his most successful novels, *The Hound of the Baskervilles.* In 1980, Umberto Eco gave Baskerville's name to a character in his most famous novel, *The Name of the Rose.*

Baskerville moved to the bottom of the page all the marginal notes of the original King James Bible. Only the Bible's chronology can be found in the margins of the 1763 folio.

The Bible was printed in 1,250 copies and part of the press run was sold by subscription. A list of subscribers including almost 300 names is bound with the Bible. At least five of the subscribers were Americans: the Virginians Thomas Adams, Charles Carter, Colonel William Diggs, and Colonel George Mercer, and the New Englander Thomas Aptthorp of Boston. Adams (1730–1788) represented Virginia at the Continental Congress and signed the Articles of Confederation.

The Bible is open to show its beautiful title page. Fig, 30.1 shows the beginning of the Psalter.

THE NEW
TESTAMENT

OF OUR

LORD and SAVIOUR

JESUS CHRIST,

Tranſlated out of the

ORIGINAL GREEK:

AND

With the former TRANSLATIONS

Diligently Compared and Reviſed,

By His MAJESTY's Special Command.

Appointed to be read in CHURCHES.

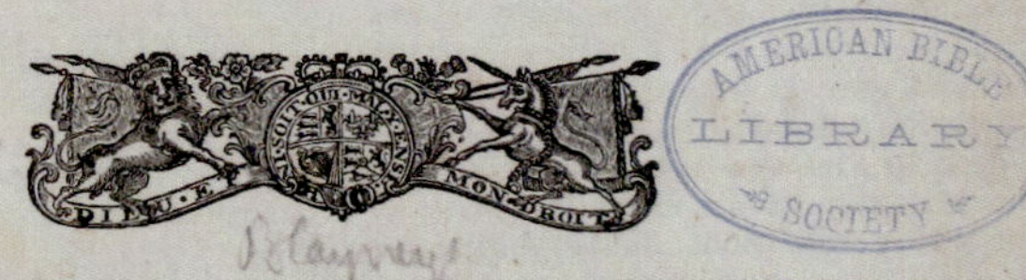

OXFORD,

Printed by *T. Wright* and *W. Gill*, Printers to the UNIVERSITY:

And ſold by *R. Baldwin* and *S. Crowder*, in Paternoſter Row, London; and by

W. Jackſon, in the High Street, Oxford. 1769.

CUM PRIVILEGIO.

31. Bible with Apocrypha

31. Bible with
Apocrypha

Oxford: T. Wright and W. Gill, 1769

4°: a² b⁴, A-6K⁴, A-2A⁴, 5L-6Z⁴; 654 ff. 250 x 185 mm. Herbert 1196

Not to be outdone by its rival, the University of Oxford issued its own scholarly text of the King James Bible within years of the Cambridge edition. The editor of the Oxford standard text was Benjamin Blayney (1728–1801), a scholar who specialized in Hebrew. Having successfully seen through the press both the quarto and the folio Bibles, in October 1769 Blayney submitted to the University's Delegates a full "account of the collation and revision" of the text[73] starting with the editions he had used and ending with details about the printing process. It appears that Blayney had spent between three and four years working on the new Oxford text and had collated the 1611 folio with the Bible published in 1701 "under the direction of Bishop Lloyd," and "two Cambridge editions of late date," a quarto and an octavo. The 1701 Bible is usually identified with the London edition (see Cat. 27), but may as well be the Oxford edition listed as Herbert 867. Of the two Cambridge editions, the quarto was probably the first 1762 Parris edition, listed as Herbert 1143, and the octavo is believed to be a Bible published in 1765, listed as Herbert 1162. The Cambridge editions published in 1767 and 1768 were probably too late to be of any use to Blayney. One wonders why he did not select the 1762 folio. Blayney acknowledges the contributions of two other Cambridge scholars, Mr. Griffith and Mr. Wheeler. His revision resulted in a more consistent use of italics to indicate words added by the translators, an expanded list of marginal references, corrections made to the running titles and chapter summaries, and not a few emendations of the translation itself.[74]

Blayney's report makes it clear that in 1769 the folio edition was printed after the quarto and may include a few corrections. When describing the printing process, Blayney starts by writing: "In this state the Quarto Copy was sent to the press." The phrase suggests that the printers' copy was a printed quarto edition of the Bible, presumably the 1762 Cambridge quarto, with corrections and additions written by hand by Blayney himself and the scholars who helped him. The forms used to print the quarto were enlarged to produce the folio, a process that was far more complicated than Blayney had anticipated and entailed a complete revision of the marginal notes and running titles. The Bible is open to show its title page.

73. The text was reprinted by Norton (2005: 195–97).

74. Norton 2005: 107–114

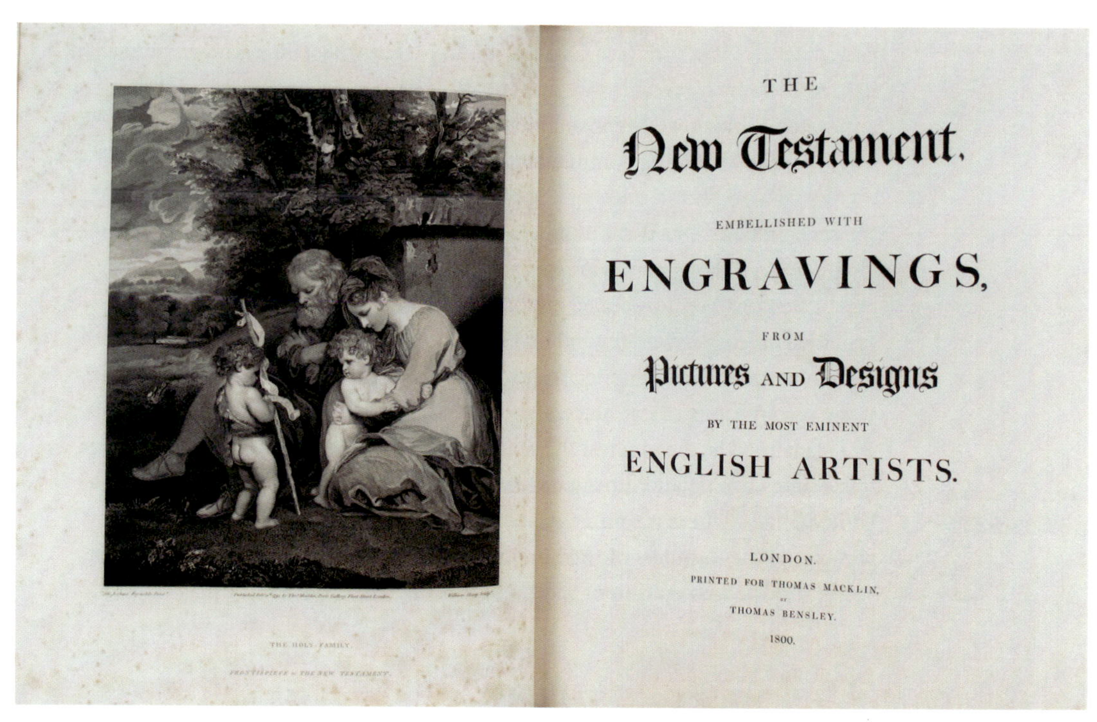

THE
New Testament,

EMBELLISHED WITH

ENGRAVINGS,

FROM

Pictures AND Designs

BY THE MOST EMINENT

ENGLISH ARTISTS.

LONDON.
PRINTED FOR THOMAS MACKLIN,
BY
THOMAS BENSLEY.
1800.

33. Bible

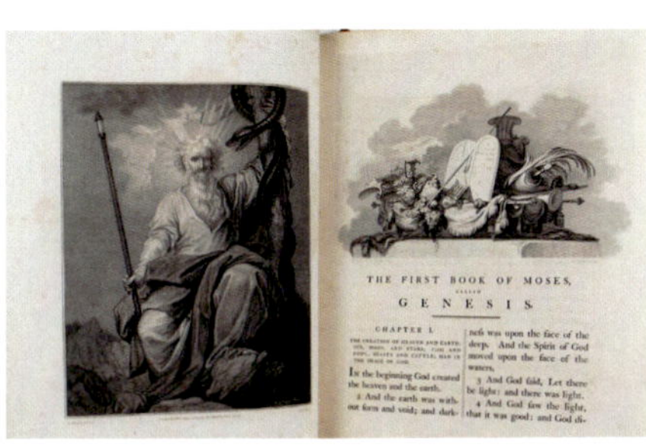

Fig. 33.1

This Bible of colossal dimensions was the last work of Thomas Macklin (1752/3–1800), a print seller and picture dealer better known for his *Poet's Gallery,* a collection of engravings based on some 100 original paintings he had commissioned in the late 1780s. Oxford University Press refused to grant Macklin permission to print the text of the King James Bible, but he managed to circumvent their opposition by including a minimal number of footnotes printed in microscopic type way below the text and implying he was publishing a Bible commentary. In most copies, including the one on display, the bottom portion of the printed pages was cut off during the process of binding and the notes disappeared completely.[76]

Macklin's Bible is remarkable for its sheer size, its illustrations, and its typography. The text is embellished with 71 plates engraved after original art work by noted artists Joshua Reynolds, Angelica Kaufmann, Philippe Jacques de Louthenbourg, and others. For the frontispiece of the New Testament, shown here, Macklin commissioned from Reynolds a depiction of the Holy Family and paid him 500 pounds. He spent an estimated 30,000 pounds for the whole Bible. Macklin had a list of 703 subscribers including George III and several members of the royal family. Four Americans were subscribers, among them Thomas Dobson, the Philadelphia printer who produced the first American editions of the *Encyclopaedia Britannica* and the Hebrew Bible.

Macklin used the best available paper and a specially designed large-size font. The pages of his Bible have a rarefied appearance with generous margins and only 29 lines to a full column. The text fills six huge volumes even though Macklin dropped the original dedication to King James, the translators' preface, the Apocrypha, and the marginal notes. Surprisingly, his font includes the long *s* that was practically out of use in England by the year 1800. To indicate the presence of words not found in the original Hebrew and Greek texts, Macklin did not use italics, as was the common practice in all roman-type editions since 1612. Instead he placed an almost invisible dot under their first vowel.

When Macklin died, in October 1800, the printing of his Bible was almost completed. His six-volume set remains the largest printed edition of the King James Bible. Fig. 33.1 shows the opening of Genesis.

76. See De Hamel 2001: 255–256

IV. The King James Bible in America (1782–1800)

The English Bible came to America as a prized possession of the earliest colonists. The settlers of Jamestown probably owned copies of the Bishops' Bible, while the Pilgrims who landed in Plymouth brought into the New World copies of the Geneva Bible. The King James Bible replaced both earlier versions within years of its first publication. The last complete Bible in the Bishops' version was issued in 1602 and the last British edition of the Geneva Bible dates from 1616. Copies of earlier editions continued to be used and pirate editions of the Geneva Bible were produced in Amsterdam until 1644, but they fought a losing battle against the King James Bible.

The King James text was published in London since 1611, in Cambridge since 1629, in Edinburgh since 1633, and in Oxford since 1679. The American colonists were never granted permission to publish it. As long as Bibles printed in England or in Amsterdam were readily available on the American market, there was little interest in producing locally the King James Bible. The Revolutionary War changed the situation radically by obstructing the import of English Bibles from Europe while also suppressing the need for a royal license to print them in America.

Robert Aitken (1734–1802), a Scottish immigrant who had come to Philadelphia in 1771, realized the time had come to publish an American edition of the King James text. The Bible he released in 1782 remained the only English Bible printed in America for the next eight years. The 1790s became a turning point in the history of Bible printing in the United States. The number of printers who produced entire Bibles or separate editions of the New Testament increased exponentially and their location covered a large area of the New Republic, from Trenton in New Jersey, to Worcester in Massachusetts or to New York and from Wilmington in Delaware to Exeter in New Hampshire. At the same time, the format of the Bibles became more diverse with deluxe illustrated editions being offered in addition to more affordable and smaller Bibles. The most significant editions of the King James Bible printed in America prior to 1800 are discussed in this chapter.

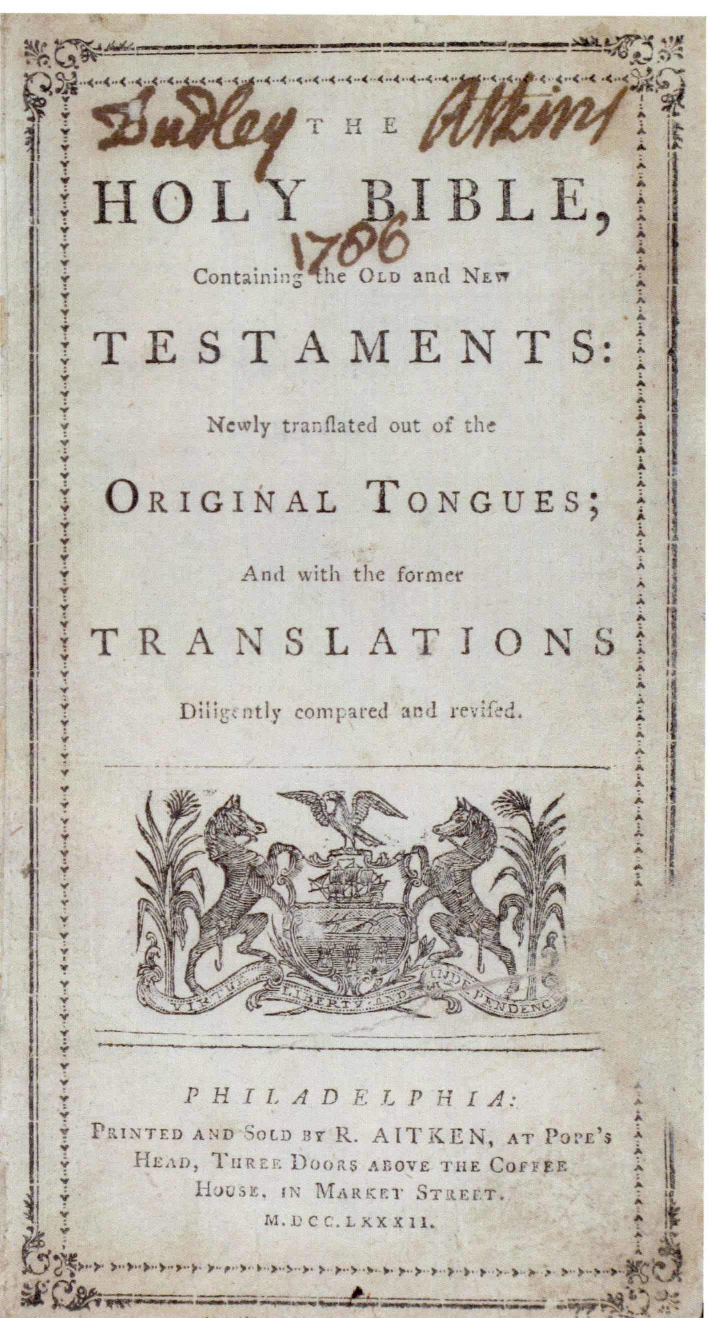

THE HOLY BIBLE,

Containing the OLD and NEW

TESTAMENTS:

Newly translated out of the

ORIGINAL TONGUES;

And with the former

TRANSLATIONS

Diligently compared and revised.

PHILADELPHIA:

PRINTED AND SOLD BY R. AITKEN, AT POPE'S HEAD, THREE DOORS ABOVE THE COFFEE HOUSE, IN MARKET STREET. M.DCC.LXXXII.

34. Bible

Philadelphia: Robert Aitken, 1782–81

12°: A-2Z¹² 3A³ A-U⁶ W-2D⁶; 736 ff. 143 x 80 mm. Hills 11

Aitken started by issuing a small size New Testament in 1777, which proved a commercial success and went through two more printings in 1778 and 1779. At the time, he was printer to the Continental Congress and had a prosperous business. Encouraged by the reception of his New Testament, he started printing a slightly larger duodecimo edition of the entire Bible in 1781 and completed it in 1782. Aitken had already obtained from Congress a resolution praising his Bible as a "pious and laudable undertaking … subservient to the interest of religion" and "an instance of the progress of arts" in America. It was the first time Congress had recommended a Bible and was to remain the last. Aitken was allowed to reprint the laudatory document as a sort of preface to his edition. Unfortunately for him, by the time he released the Bible, commercial ties with Europe had resumed and the American market was flooded with King James Bibles produced in England. Aitken had printed about 10,000 copies and his sales did not cover his costs. The Presbyterian Synod of Pennsylvania saved him from bankruptcy by purchasing many copies for charitable distribution among the poor, but his business never recovered its earlier status. Perhaps Aitken's most esteemed supporter was President George Washington, who expressed his willingness to provide a copy of the Bible to each combatant. The plan came to nothing because most of the troops were demobilized before Aitken could complete the printing of his edition.

Aitken did not include the Apocrypha in his Bible, perhaps in order to save on the cost of printing. He indicated his address on the title page as was customary at the time and as a way to stimulate sales: "Philadelphia, Printed and Sold by R. Aitken, at Pope's Head, Three Doors above the Coffee House, in Market Street." Of the considerable number of copies he printed, fewer than 40 survive. About 30 of them, including the two copies in the Rare Bible Collection @ MOBIA, are in institutional or public libraries, while five to ten remain in private hands. The Bible is open at its title page.

s into committees, to each of
not only with the best tranſla
gs of the Original text. Aft
ted the parts aſſigned the
on newly formed, the reſt ha
ae ancient verſions, and when
it was determined what wa
firſt publiſhed A. D. 1610, a
blic authority, and generall
y, that it has been generally
, of which its having never
ears, is a ſufficient proof
from one of the lateſt and
een diſcovered in that, have be

Writing the Books
ENT.

	Years from the death of Chriſt.	Years birth
	6	
	10	
	19	
	19	
	23	
Romans,	23	
eſians, and	24	
	29	
	30	
and the 2d,		
	30	
	61	
	63	
s and that of	65	
	38	

Books of the OLD T
of their Chapters.

Chap. 36	Daniel hath Chapters
10	Hoſea
13	Joel
10	Amos
42	Obadiah
150	Jonah
31	Micah
12	Nahum
8	Habakkuk
66	Zephaniah
52	Haggai
5	Zechariah
48	Malachi

TESTAMENT.

ers	6	Hebrews hath Chap
	4	The Epiſtle of James
	4	I. Peter
	5	II. Peter
	3	I. John
	6	II. John
	4	III. John
	3	Jude
	1	Revelation

¶ The First Book of MOSES,
CALLED
GENESIS.

CHAP. I.

1 The creation of heaven and earth, 3 of the light, 6 of the firmament, 9 of the earth ſeparated from the waters, 11 and made fruitful, 14 of the ſun, moon, and ſtars, 20 of ſiſh and fowl, 24 of beaſts and cattle, 26 of man in the image of God; 29 alſo the appointment of food.

IN the beginning God created the heaven and the earth.

2 And the earth was without form, and void; and darkneſs was upon the face of the deep: and the Spirit of God moved upon the face of the waters.

3 ¶ And God ſaid, Let there be light: and there was light.

4 And God ſaw the light, that *it was* good: and God divided the light from the darkneſs.

5 And God called the light Day, and the darkneſs he called Night. And the evening and the morning were the firſt day.

6 ¶ And God ſaid, Let there be a firmament in the midſt of the waters, and let it divide the the waters from the waters.

7 And God made the firmament, and divided the waters which *were* under the firmament from the waters which *were* above the firmament: and it was ſo.

8 And God called the firmament Heaven. And the evening and the morning were the ſecond day.

9 ¶ And God ſaid, Let the waters under the heaven be gathered together unto one place, and let the dry *land* appear: and it was ſo.

10 And God called the dry *land* Earth, and the gathering together of the waters called he Seas: and God ſaw that *it was* good.

11 And God ſaid, Let the earth bring forth graſs, the herb yielding ſeed, *and* the fruit-tree yielding fruit after his kind, whoſe ſeed *is* in itſelf, upon the earth: and it was ſo.

12 And the earth brought forth graſs, *and* herb yielding ſeed after his kind, and the tree yielding fruit, whoſe ſeed *was* in itſelf, after his kind: and God ſaw that *it was* good.

13 And the evening and the morning were the third day.

14 ¶ And God ſaid, Let there be lights in the firmament of the heaven, to divide the day from the night: and let them be for ſigns, and for ſeaſons, and for days, and years.

15 And let them be for lights in the firmament of the heaven, to give light upon the earth: and it was ſo.

16 And God made two great lights; the greater light to rule the day, and the leſſer light to rule the night: *he* made the ſtars alſo.

17 And God ſet them in the firmament of the heaven, to give light upon the earth,

18 And to rule over the day, and over the night, and to divide the light from the darkneſs: and God ſaw that *it was* good.

19 And the evening and the morning were the fourth day.

20 ¶ And God ſaid, Let the waters bring forth abundantly the moving creature that hath life, and fowl *that* may fly above the earth in the open firmament of heaven.

21 And God created great whales, and every living creature that moveth, which the waters brought forth abundantly after their kind, and every winged fowl after his kind: and God ſaw that *it was* good.

22 And God bleſſed them, ſaying, Be fruitful, and multiply, and fill the waters in the ſeas, and let fowl multiply in the earth.

23 And the evening and the morning were the fifth day.

24 ¶ And God ſaid, Let the earth bring forth the living creature after his kind, cattle, and creeping thing, and beaſt of the earth after his kind: and it was ſo.

25 And God made the beaſt of the earth after his kind, and cattle after their kind, and every thing that creepeth upon the earth after his kind: and God ſaw that *it was* good.

26 ¶ And God ſaid, Let us make man in our image, after our likeneſs; and let them have dominion over the fiſh of the ſea, and over the fowl of the air, and over the cattle, and over all the earth, and over every creeping thing that creepeth upon the earth.

27 So God created man in his *own* image; in the image of God created he him: male and female created he them.

28 And God bleſſed them; and God ſaid unto them, Be fruitful, and multiply, and repleniſh the earth, and ſubdue it: and have dominion over the fiſh of the ſea, and over the fowl of the air, and over every living thing that moveth upon the earth.

29 ¶ And God ſaid, Behold, I have given you every herb bearing ſeed, which *is* upon the face of all the earth, and every tree, in the which *is* the fruit of a tree yielding ſeed; to you it ſhall be for meat.

30 And to every beaſt of the earth, and to every fowl of the air, and to every thing that creepeth upon the earth, wherein *there is* life, *I have given* every green herb for meat: and it was ſo.

31 And God ſaw every thing that he had made, and, behold, *it was* very good. And the evening and the morning were the ſixth day.

CHAP. II.

1 The firſt ſabbath. 8 The garden of Eden. 17 The tree of knowledge. 19, 20 The creatures named. 21 Women made, and marriage inſtituted.

THus the heavens and the earth were finiſhed, and all the hoſt of them.

2 And on the ſeventh day God ended his work which he had made: and he reſted on the ſeventh day from all his work which he had made.

3 And

35. Bible | PHILADELPHIA: WILLIAM YOUNG, 1790

12°: A-2L¹², A-E⁶ F⁵; 443 ff. 153 x 88 mm. Hills 25

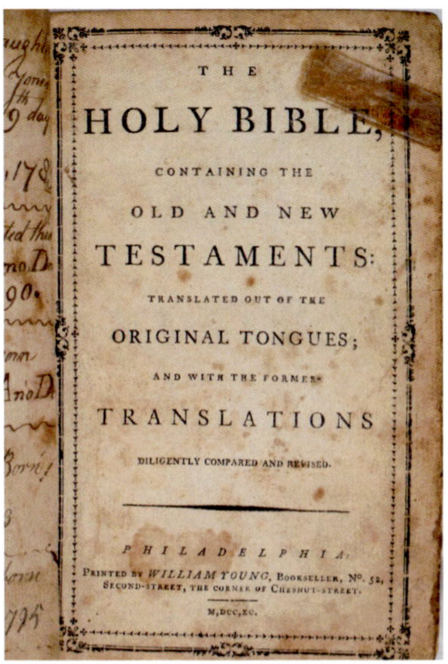

Fig. 35.1

After Aitken's financial debacle, no complete English Bible was published in the United States until 1790, when two different editions were released in Philadelphia. The first one was printed by the Irish refugee Matthew Carey (1760–1839) and is remembered as the first Catholic Bible produced in the New World. The one described here was the second American edition of the King James text. It was published by William Young (1755–1829), a Scottish immigrant who had come to Philadelphia in June 1784 and opened there his own printing shop and book store. Between 1790 and 1808, Young released five duodecimo editions of the entire Bible and at least two editions of the New Testament. His Bibles, like Aitken's duodecimo, lack the Apocrypha. Young kept his costs low by using a font slightly smaller than Aitken's and cramming 73 lines of text into each full column. He needed only 40 sheets of paper for each copy of the Bible. Aitken's Bible had only 50 lines to a full column, but filled 61 sheets of paper per copy.

In 1790, Young also printed the Scottish version of the *Metrical Psalms* that was commonly used in the Presbyterian Church and bound part of the edition as an appendix to his Bible. Years later he managed to sell the remaining copies to Matthew Carey who bound them with his own edition of the Bible in 1817.[77]

77. Hills 333

Young's Bible is open at the beginning of Genesis. Fig. 35.1 shows its title page.

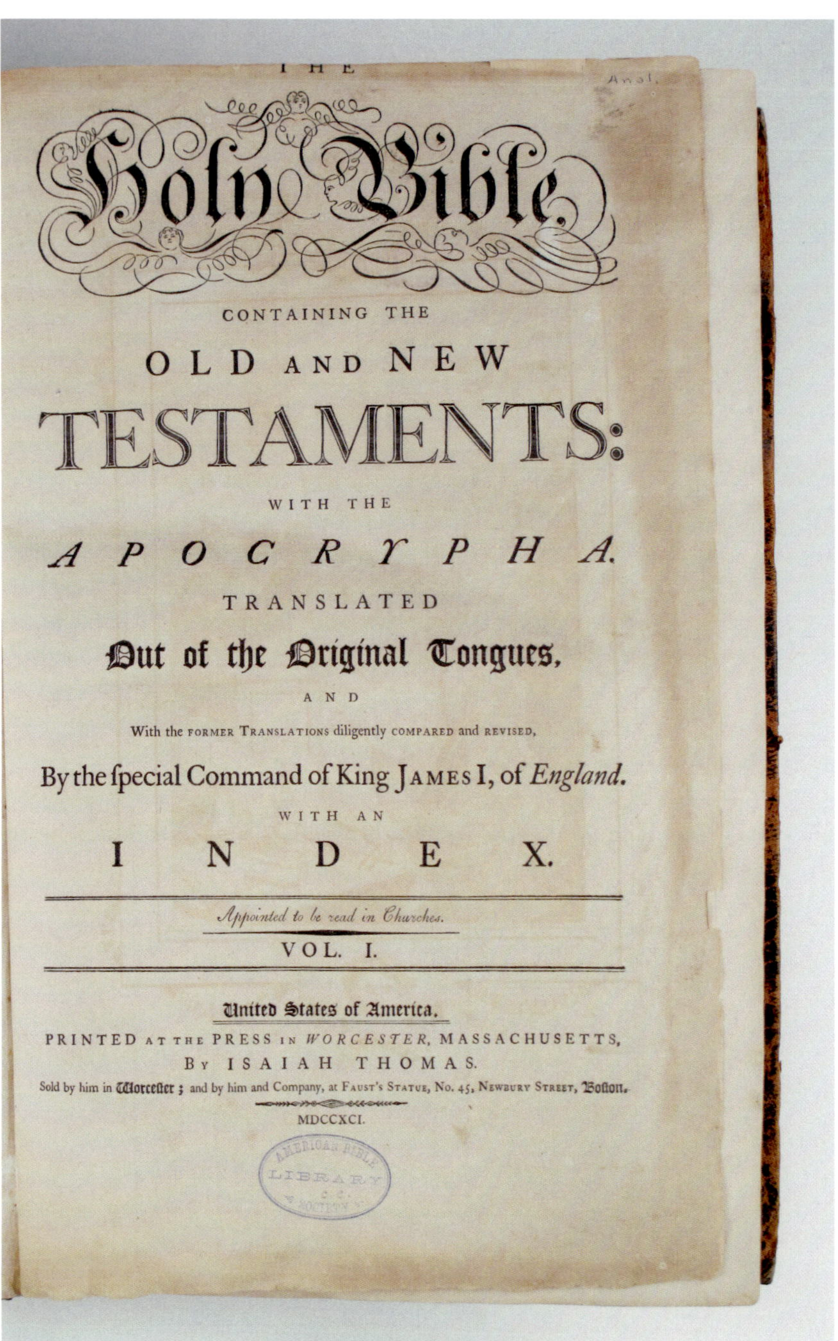

36. Bible with Apocrypha

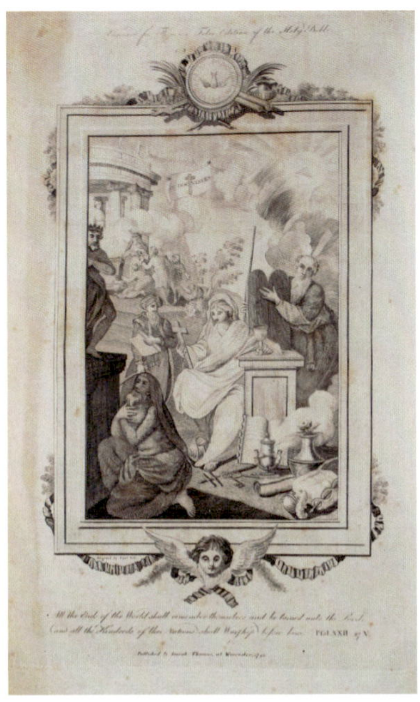

Fig. 36.1

While Aitken and Young had printed modest duodecimo Bibles, Isaiah Thomas (1750–1831) was the first American printer to produce a deluxe edition of the King James text. Acclaimed by its contemporaries as the most beautiful book printed in America, it was both the first folio and the first illustrated Bible crafted in the New World. Thomas had built a solid reputation as a patriot during the Revolutionary War and was one of the most important printers and publishers of the new Republic. He started his career as a six-year-old apprentice and during his long professional life he produced over 900 books, edited newspapers and almanacs, founded the American Antiquarian Society, and authored the *History of Printing in America,* a monograph still used today.

To enhance the quality of his publications, Thomas built his own paper mill and bindery. He made sure the text of his Bible was correct by examining some 30 different editions of the King James Version. He enlisted as proof readers "Clergymen of Worcester and … other capable persons" and managed to complete the whole press run in one year. To illustrate the Bible, he commissioned four New England artists to produce 50 copper plate engravings. Designed in the rococo style much favored during the Enlightenment, these images were meant to add a note of refinement to the printed volumes and make them more attractive.[78] Thomas used the same plates for the folio edition and the more affordable quarto he released the same year.[79] He issued the following advertisement for the quarto edition: "The price to subscribers … shall be only Seven Dollars … the Publisher will receive one half of the sum, or twenty-one shillings, in the following articles, viz. Wheat, Rye, Indian Corn, or Pork…" .

The Bible is open to show both its title page and its frontispiece (Fig. 36.1).

78. Gutjahr 1999: 47–56

79. Hills 30

THE

HOLY BIBLE,

CONTAINING THE

OLD AND NEW

TESTAMENTS:

TRANSLATED OUT OF THE

ORIGINAL TONGUES:

AND WITH THE FORMER

TRANSLATIONS

Diligently compared and revifed.

TRENTON:

PRINTED AND SOLD BY ISAAC COLLINS.

M.DCC.XCI.

37. Bible with Apocrypha

<table>
<tr><td>

37. Bible with
Apocrypha

</td><td>

TRENTON: ISAAC COLLINS, 1791

4°: A-4Q⁴ 4R², A-U⁴, A-2G⁴ 2H², A-T⁴; 658 ff. 247 x 177 mm. Hills 31

</td></tr>
</table>

80. Hixson 1968: 137–157

In 1789, when Isaac Collins (1746–1817) decided to publish a quarto edition of the King James Bible, he was already an experienced printer and had issued at least four editions of the New Testament. For his Bible,[80] Collins offered an attractive payment plan to potential subscribers, as did his competitor, Isaiah Thomas. Collins' initial plan was to attract 3,000 orders. To stimulate sales, he announced, in 1790 or 1791, that he would add to the biblical text a reprint of the popular concordance compiled by John Downame (d. 1652) in 1631. He targeted "all Protestant denominations and was prepared to customize his Bible according to specific requests. For radicals who objected to the inclusion of the Apocrypha or to the end notes authored by the Swiss theologian Jean-Frédéric Ostervald (1663–1747), Collins was willing to issue Bibles consisting of the Old and New Testaments alone. His project was endorsed by the Presbyterians, the Episcopalians, and the Baptists, not to mention his fellow Quakers, who purchased four-fifths of the 5,000 copies he finally printed.

81. Herbert 1295

Collins showed more concern for the accuracy of the printed text than any other contemporary American publisher, including Isaiah Thomas. His Bible was reprinted page for page from the Oxford quarto edition of 1784,[81] as he had advertised in 1789, but the proofs were read against three other quartos published in Cambridge in 1668, in London in 1772, and in Edinburgh in 1775. When the four English texts did not agree, Collins consulted scholars able to check them with the original Hebrew and Greek readings. To make sure no errors remained in his printed Bible, Collins used his own children as proofreaders and rewarded them with a pound for every misprint they detected. They went through the proofs 11 times and missed only one broken letter and a misplaced punctuation mark. Collins' Bible earned a well-merited reputation for correctness and was used as printer's copy by many publishers, including Matthew Carey.

None of the early American editions of the King James Bible includes the dedication to King James and the original preface written by Miles Smith. Collins replaced these texts with a new foreword written by John Witherspoon (1723–1794), the President of Princeton University and the only clergyman who signed the Declaration of Independence. Including useful information about the history of Bible translation, Witherspoon's preface soon became popular and was frequently reprinted throughout the nineteenth century.

Collins' Bible is open to show its title page.

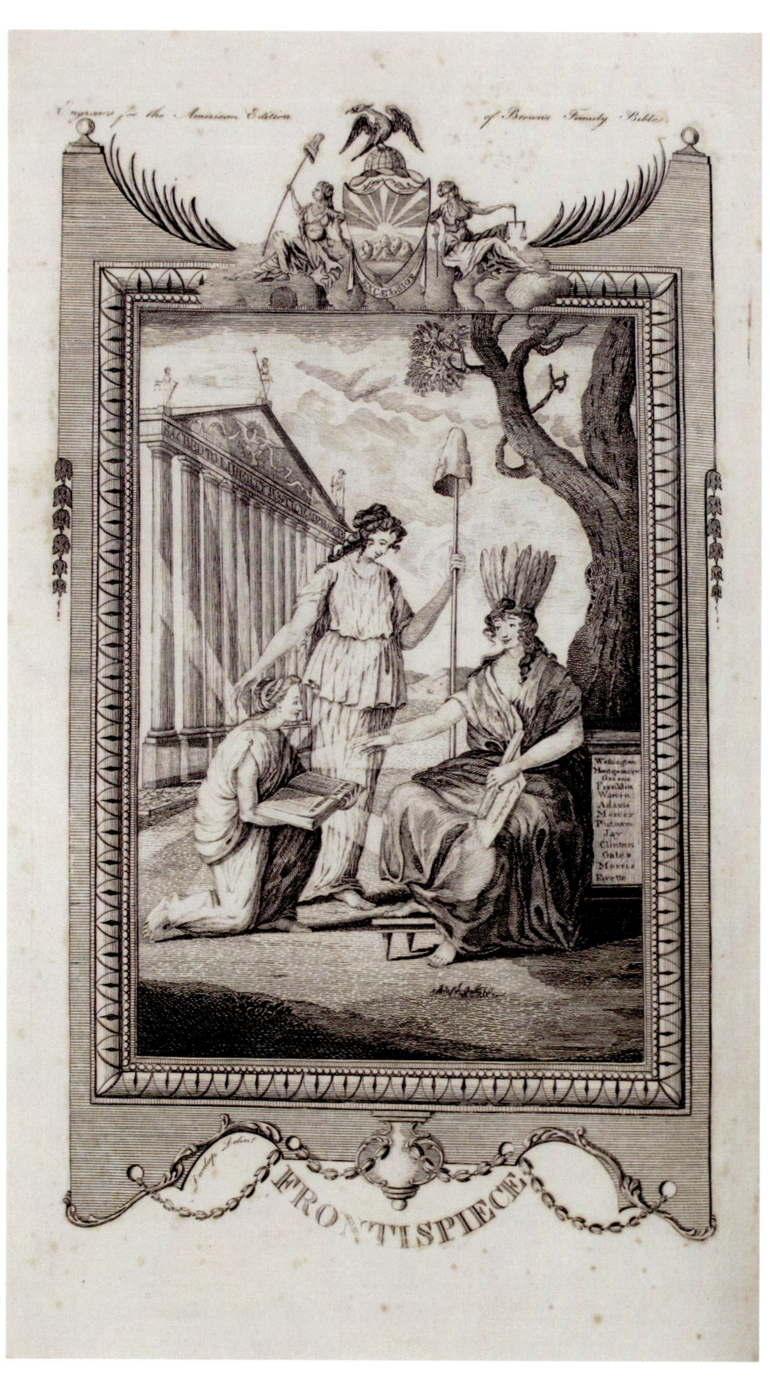

38. Self-Interpreting Bible

NEW YORK: HODGE AND CAMPBELL, 1792

2°: π² a-k², A-8A², [A-T²], A-3X², [6]; 390 [+38] ff. 376 x 213 mm. Hills 37

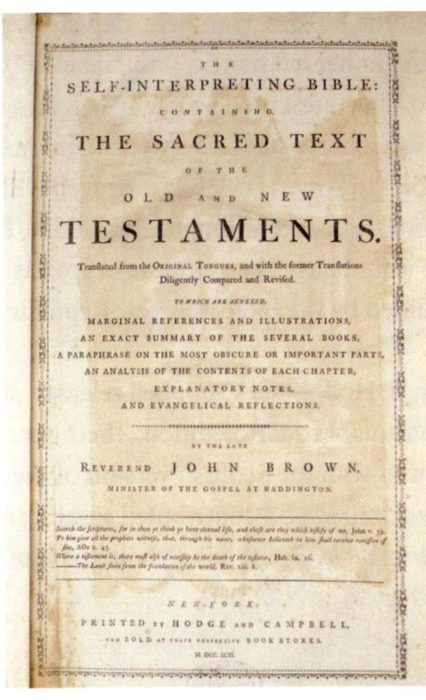

Fig. 38.1

Completed in April 1792, this was the first Bible printed in New York and the second folio Bible produced in America. Its publication was approved in April 1790 by the New York State Senate and Assembly in a resolution that praised the printers for promoting "the Industry and Manufactures of America" and expressed the hope that they "may meet sufficient encouragement to complete their undertaking … whereby the people may be supplied with this edition much cheaper than can be imported."

One month later, the two publishers, Robert Hodge (1746–1813) and Samuel Campbell (1763?–1836), started distributing a prospectus that promoted the Bible to potential subscribers. Their folio was to be "a genuine American edition" of a Bible first published in Edinburgh in 1778 and "the largest and cheapest ever proposed to be printed in the United States."[82] In addition to the introduction, notes, and extensive comments prepared by John Brown (1722–1787) for the Scottish edition, the *Self-Interpreting Bible* issued by Hodge and Campbell also included Witherspoon's preface borrowed from Collins' Bible (Cat. 37) and 19 full-page illustrations specially engraved for the American edition.

As indicated in the prospectus, the Bible was printed in 40 installments or "numbers" over a period of two years. The price for subscribers was 25 cents per number with a free number added to every group of 12. The section including the Apocrypha, printed in a smaller type, was available upon demand. A list of subscribers was distributed with the last number. It includes about 1,300 names and provides a cross section of American society and life. George Washington is listed as the first subscriber, but next to him, in alphabetical order, we find carpenters, shoe makers, stone-cutters, a door-opener to Congress, masons, weavers, Supreme Court Justice John Jay, William Samuel Johnson, the President of Columbia College, a wheelwright and a chair maker, several ladies, the Hon. Henry Knox "Secretary at War", a sail-maker, a tailor, and many, many more. In years to come, three of the subscribers would become officers of the American Bible Society: John Jay and Richard Varick, the Society's second and third Presidents, and John Pintard, its Recording Secretary.

82. Wright 1894: 102–105

THE

FIRST BOOK of MOSES,

CALLED

GENESIS.

CHAPTER I.

1 The creation of heaven and earth, 3 of the light, 6 of the firmament, 9 of the earth separated from the waters, 11 and made fruitful, 14 of the sun, moon, and stars, 20 of fish and fowl, 24 of beasts and cattle, 26 of man in the image of God. 29 Also the appointment of food.

IN the a beginning God created the heaven and the earth.

2 And the earth was without form, and void; and darknefs *was* upon the face of the deep: and the Spirit of God moved upon the face of the waters.

3 And God faid, b Let there be light: and there was light.

4 And God faw the light, that *it was* good: and God divided † the light from the darknefs.

5 And God called the light Day, and the darknefs he called Night: † and the evening and the morning were the firft day.

6 ¶ And God faid, c Let there be a † firmament in the midft of the waters, and let it divide the waters from the waters.

7 And God made the firmament; and divided the waters which *were* under the firmament from the waters which *were* above the firmament: and it was fo.

8 And God called the d firmament Heaven: and the evening and the morning were the fecond day.

9 ¶ And God faid, e Let the waters under the heaven be gathered together unto one place, and let the dry *land* appear: and it was fo.

10 And God called the dry *land* Earth, and the gathering together of the waters called he Seas: and God faw that *it was* good.

11 And God faid, Let the earth bring forth † grafs, the herb yielding feed, *and* the fruit-tree yielding fruit after his kind, whofe feed *is* in itfelf, upon the earth: and it was fo.

12 And the earth brought forth grafs, *and* herb yielding feed after his kind, and the tree yielding fruit, whofe feed *was* in itfelf, after his kind: and God faw that *it was* good.

13 And the evening and the morning were the third day.

14 ¶ And God faid, Let there be f lights in the firmament of the heaven, to divide † the day from the night: and let them be for figns, and for feafons, and for days, and years.

15 And let them be for lights in the firmament of the heaven, to give light upon the earth: and it was fo.

16 And God made two great lights; the greater light † to rule the day, and the leffer light to rule the night: *he made* the ftars alfo.

17 And God fet them in the firmament of the heaven to give light upon the earth:

18 And to g rule over the day, and over the night, and to divide the light from the darknefs: and God faw that *it was* good.

19 And the evening and the morning were the fourth day.

20 And God faid, h Let the waters bring forth abundantly the ‖ moving creature that hath † life, and fowl *that* may fly above the earth in the † open firmament of heaven.

21 And God created great whales, and every living creature that moveth, which the waters brought forth abundantly after their kind, and every winged fowl after his kind: and God faw that *it was* good.

22 And God bleffed them, faying, i Be fruitful, and multiply, and fill the waters in the feas, and let fowl multiply in the earth.

23 And the evening and the morning were the fifth day.

24 ¶ And God faid, Let the earth bring forth the living creature after his kind, cattle, and creeping thing, and beaft of the earth after his kind: and it was fo.

25 And God made the beaft of the earth after his kind, and cattle after their kind, and every thing that creepeth upon the earth after his kind: and God faw that *it was* good.

26 ¶ And God faid, k Let us make man in our image, after our likenefs: and let them have dominion over the fifh of the fea, and over the fowl of the air, and over the cattle, and over all the earth, and over every creeping thing that creepeth upon the earth.

27 So God created man in his *own* image, in the image of God created he him; l male and female created he them.

28 And God bleffed them, and God faid unto them, m Be fruitful, and multiply, and replenifh the earth, and fubdue it: and have dominion over the fifh of the fea, and over the fowl of the air, and over every living thing that † moveth upon the earth.

29 ¶ And God faid, Behold, I have given you every herb † bearing feed, which *is* upon the face of all the earth, and every tree, in the which *is* the fruit of a tree yielding feed; n to you it fhall be for meat.

30 And to every beaft of the earth, and to every fowl of the air, and to every thing that creepeth upon the earth, wherein *there is* † life, *I have given* every green herb for meat: and it was fo.

31 And o God faw every thing that he had made, and behold, *it was* very good. And the evening and the morning were the fixth day.

CHAPTER II.

1 The firft fabbath. 4 The manner of the creation. 8 The planting of the garden of Eden, 10 and the river thereof. 17 The tree of knowledge only forbidden. 19, 20 The naming of the creatures. 21 The making of woman, and inftitution of marriage.

THUS the heavens and the earth were finifhed, and all the hoft of them.

2 a And on the feventh day God ended his work which he had made; and he refted on the feventh day from all his work which he had made.

3 And God bleffed the feventh day, and fanctified it: becaufe that in it he had refted from all his work which God † created and made.

4 ¶ Thefe *are* the generations of the heavens and of the earth when they were created, in the day that the LORD God made the earth and the heavens,

5 And every plant of the field before it was in the earth, and every herb of the field before it grew: for the LORD God had not caufed it to rain upon the earth, and *there was* not a man to till the ground.

6 But ‖ there went up a mift from the earth, and watered the whole face of the ground.

7 And the LORD God formed man † *of* the b duft of the ground, and breathed into his noftrils the breath of life; and c man became a living foul.

B

8 ¶ And

PHILADELPHIA: JACOB R. BERRIMAN FOR BERRIMAN & CO., 1796

2°: A–9D²; 376 ff. 363 x 216 mm. Hills 53

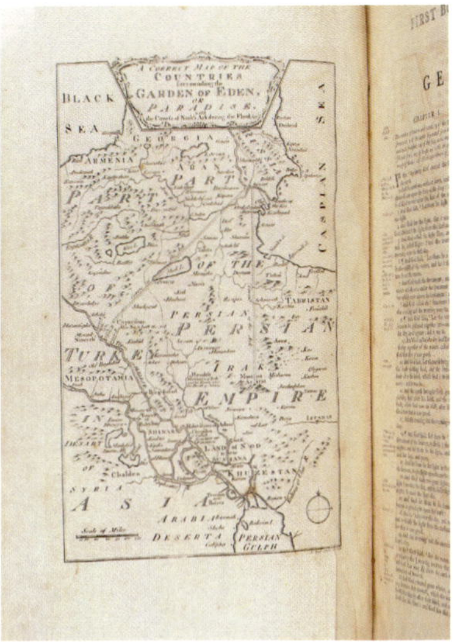

Fig. 39.1

This is the third folio Bible printed in America and the first one to be issued in Philadelphia. It does not include any prefatory material, but at the end of Revelation it has the *Index to the Holy Bible* followed by the usual tables and a list of subscribers. Jacob R. Berriman was less successful than Hodge and Campbell had been a few years earlier and his list is only about half as long as theirs. Unlike his predecessors, Berriman did not print a quarto edition to accompany his folio. To provide more affordable Bibles, he simply omitted the illustrations from some of the folio copies he had printed. The 18 engravings that embellish his large folio won him high praise among the bibliophiles. The first 15 illustrate scenes from the Old Testament and include two maps. There are two illustrations in the New Testament and only one in the Apocrypha. One third of the engravings are copied from Isaiah Thomas' Bible.[83] The border was changed and the inscription mentioning Isaiah Thomas was naturally dropped, but the images are identical, though executed by different artists. *Gideon's Sacrifice,* for instance, was engraved by Joseph H. Seymour for Thomas' Bible and by Cornelius Tiebout (1773–1832) for Berriman's folio.

In addition to depictions of biblical scenes, Berriman includes in his Bible a reconstruction of Solomon's Temple and two maps of the Holy Land. The Temple image was first used in Thomas' Bible and found its way into the Bible printed by Hodge and Campbell before being copied by Berriman's engraver. The *Accurate Map of the Holy Land* placed against Joshua 22–24 in the 1796 Bible was designed by Thomas Bowen (d. 1790), a celebrated map maker who has published a *Complete Atlas of Geography* in 1744–47. The Bible is open to show the beginning of Genesis with the map facing the text (Fig 39.1). According to its legend, the map represents "the Countries surrounding the Garden of Eden or Paradise, with the course of Noah's Ark during the Flood etc."

83. See O'Callaghan 1861: 51

V. The Bible Society Movement (1804–1854)

The early years of the nineteenth century ushered a new era in the history of the King James Bible. Religious leaders and concerned citizens on both sides of the Atlantic could not fail to notice that commercial publishers and book dealers were unable to supply affordable Bibles to a rapidly growing population. At the same time, the gradual replacement of manual typesetting with stereotype plates and the constant improvement of the printing presses created the possibility to mass produce Scriptures at relatively low costs. The Canstein Bible Institute established in Germany in 1710 by Karl Hildebrand von Canstein (1667–1719) had proved that affordable Scriptures could only be produced by using new technology. Between 1712 and 1719 this organization managed to print 100,000 copies of the New Testament and 40,000 copies of the entire Bible in German by employing a process that prefigured stereotyping. The Bible Society movement that started with the creation of the British and Foreign Bible Society (BFBS) in March 1804 had even more spectacular results. Within two decades it grew into a worldwide network of organizations dedicated uniquely to the printing and distribution of the Scriptures. In the United States, several local Bible Societies based on the British model were created within a few years. The Philadelphia Bible Society led the way in 1808 and was followed in 1809 by sister societies in Connecticut, Massachusetts, New York, and New Jersey. By 1816, about 100 state and community Bible Societies had been established in the United States and there was a real need for a national organization that would unify and coordinate their separate efforts. The American Bible Society, the patron of this historic collection from which *On Eagle's Wings'* is drawn, was created in May 1816, in New York.

The founding documents of the British and Foreign Bible Society specify that its "sole object shall be to encourage a wider circulation of the Holy Scriptures without note or comment" and that it will distribute only one English translation of the Bible: the Authorized Version (better known in America as the King James Version).[84] On 11 May 1816, the founders of the American Bible Society unanimously adopted a Constitution modeled on the BFBS document and including the same statement regarding the King James Bible. The constitutions of the two Societies provided the blueprint for the countless millions of English Bibles published during the next 150 years. There is no mention of the Apocrypha in these documents. The Bible Societies simply dropped this section from their editions of the King James text.

84. See Canton 1904: I 18

THE
HOLY BIBLE,

CONTAINING THE

OLD AND NEW TESTAMENTS:

TRANSLATED

OUT OF THE ORIGINAL TONGUES:

AND

WITH THE FORMER TRANSLATIONS DILIGENTLY COMPARED
AND REVISED,

By His Majesty's Special Command.

APPOINTED TO BE READ IN CHURCHES.

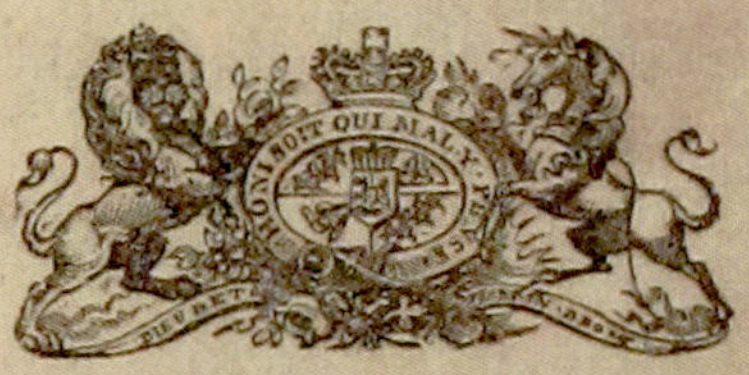

LONDON:

Printed by George Eyre and Andrew Strahan,
Printers to the King's Most Excellent Majesty,

FOR THE BRITISH AND FOREIGN BIBLE SOCIETY,
Instituted in London in the Year 1804.
And sold, to Subscribers only, by L. B. Seeley, at the
Society's Depository, No. 169, Fleet-Street.
1813.
Stereotype Edition.

 | London: Eyre and Strahan for the British and Foreign Bible Society, 1813

12°: 634, 192 p. 180 mm. Herbert 1582, cf. note on p. 326–327

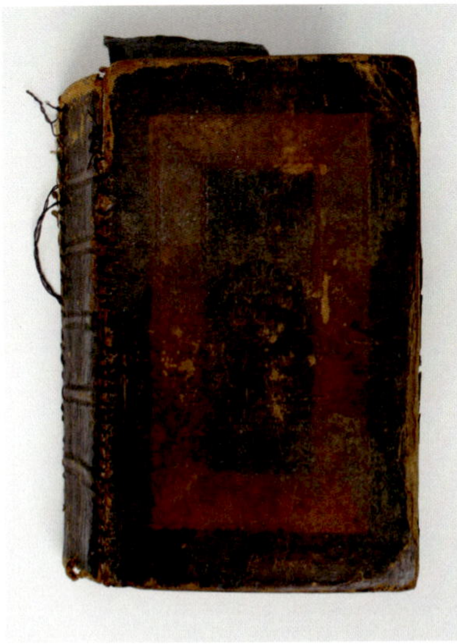

Fig. 40.1

Rather than build its own printing shop, the British and Foreign Bible Society decided to commission experienced printers to produce Scriptures under its imprint. At first the Society negotiated with Cambridge University Press and had to wait until the printers obtained stereotype plates made according to the process recently developed by Andrew Wilson. The first Bible to have the Society's name on the title page was a duodecimo edition printed in Nonpareil type in 1806, by R. Watts at Cambridge. The same year the Cambridge presses produced for the BFBS an octavo edition of the New Testament in Pica typeface.

A variety of other editions were issued regularly during the following years. By March 15, 1815, the Society had published far more copies of the King James text than any other publisher in Great Britain: 429,768 Bibles and 481,340 New Testaments.[85]

The Bible described here was printed in London from the same plates as the 1806 edition. Its price was presumably the same: 3 shillings for a copy bound in calf. The copy on display has on its fly leaf a short versified inscription composed by a certain Thomas Bailey: "This Book we give to thee / And from this school so free / That you prepared might be / To meet eternity." The handwritten text is dated: "From the Methodist Chapel Bosworth Nov. 28th 1813." The donor's name is included in the 1813 Annual Report of the British and Foreign Bible Society among the new subscribers from Liverpool.

The Bible is open to show its title page. Fig. 40.1 shows the repairs done to its binding by an unknown owner.

85. Herbert 1968: 327

THE

HOLY BIBLE,

CONTAINING THE

OLD AND NEW TESTAMENTS:

TRANSLATED

OUT OF THE ORIGINAL TONGUES,

AND

WITH THE FORMER TRANSLATIONS

DILIGENTLY COMPARED AND REVISED.

STEREOTYPE EDITION.

STEREOTYPED FOR THE

BIBLE SOCIETY AT PHILADELPHIA,

By T. RUTT, Shacklewell, London.

1812.

41. Bible

<table>
<tr><td>

45. Devotional Family Bible
</td><td>

LONDON AND NEW YORK: GEORGE VIRTUE, AFTER 1834

68 parts. 1621 p. 370 mm. Cf. Herbert 1809
</td></tr>
<tr><td>

Devotional Family Bible
</td><td>

NEW YORK: VIRTUE AND YORSTON, C. 1871

1621, 80 p. 370 mm. Cf. Hills 891, 1777, 1847
</td></tr>
</table>

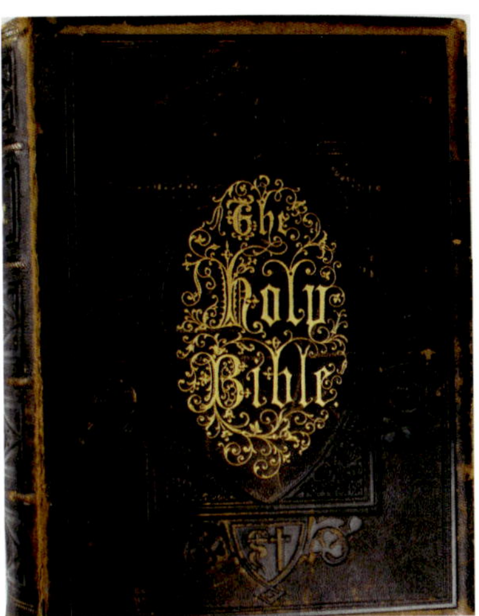

Fig. 45.1

Alexander Fletcher (1787–1860), a Scottish Presbyterian who founded in 1825 the independent and well-attended Finsbury Chapel in London, authored in 1834 a *Guide to Family Devotion* that became an instant bestseller. By the time the *Guide* had sold 40,000 copies in the United Kingdom and the United States, Fletcher was invited to edit for George Virtue and his associates a *Devotional Family Bible* that was to be even more successful than his *Guide*. Fletcher contributed to the project a vast corpus of notes meant to facilitate a "devotional reading" of the text through meditation and self-examination. Printed at the bottom of each page, these verse-by-verse reflections prefigure the format of the contemporary Life Application Bibles. The scholarly information is included in the cross-references printed between the two columns of text and in the critical notes located above the reflections. Fletcher's notes reveal the depth of his scholarship and provide useful comments on the history of the biblical text.

The publishers printed Fletcher's material on elephant folio sheets, in a beautiful font with wide margins, and embellished it with many steel engravings. Virtue (1783–1868) was well known in the English-speaking world as an unsurpassed producer of pictorial books. It appears that the *Devotional Family Bible* was first issued in 68 parts, one of which is on display. The surviving copies, whether bound or not, do not bear a date of publication and have slightly divergent imprints: George Virtue; Virtue, Emmins and Roberts; Virtue, Emmins and Company, Virtue and Yorston, etc. The British edition has 79 engravings and was probably issued for the first time in the late 1830s. Many reprints followed. The American edition, displayed here in bound form (see Fig. 45.1) has 38 engravings, most of them not borrowed from the British book. It includes two prints taken from the famous Bible illustrated by Gustave Doré that had been first published in French in 1866 and in English one year later (Cat. 47). The copy described here bears an inscription dated "Christmas 1871."

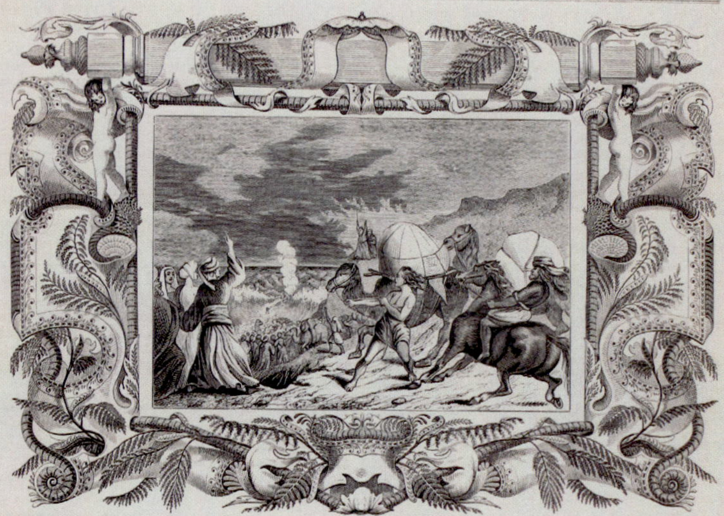

PASSAGE OF THE RED SEA.

13 And [p]every firstling of an ass thou shalt
redeem with a ||lamb; and if thou wilt not
redeem it, then thou shalt break his neck:
and all the first-born of man among thy children [q]shalt thou redeem.
14 ¶ [r]And it shall be when thy son asketh
thee †in time to come, saying, What *is* this?
that thou shalt say unto him, [s]By strength of
hand the LORD brought us out from Egypt,
from the house of bondage:
15 And it came to pass, when Pharaoh
would hardly let us go, that [t]the LORD slew
all the first-born in the land of Egypt, both
the first-born of man, and the first-born of
beast: therefore I sacrifice to the LORD all
that openeth the matrix, being males; but all
the first-born of my children I redeem.
16 And it shall be for [u]a token upon thine
hand, and for frontlets between thine eyes:
for by strength of hand the LORD brought us
forth out of Egypt.
17 ¶ And it came to pass, when Pharaoh
had let the people go, that God led them not
through the way of the land of the Philis-
tines, although that *was* near; for God said,
Lest peradventure the people [x]repent when
they see war, and [y]they return to Egypt:
18 But God [z]led the people about, *through*
the way of the wilderness of the Red Sea:
and the children of Israel went up ||harness-
ed out of the land of Egypt.
19 And Moses took the bones of Joseph
with him: for he had straitly sworn the children of Israel, saying, [a]God will surely visit
you; and ye shall carry up my bones away
hence with you.

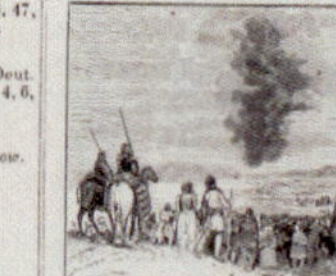

20 ¶ And [b]they took
their journey from
Succoth, and en-
camped in Etham, in
the edge of the wil-
derness.
21 And [c]the LORD
went before them by
day in a pillar of a
cloud, to lead them
the way; and by night in a pillar of fire, to
give them light: to go by day and night.
22 He took not away the pillar of the cloud
by day, nor the pillar of fire by night, *from*
before the people.

B.C. 1491.

p ch. 34, 20. Numbers 18, 15, 16.
|| Or, *kid*.
q Numb. 3. 46, 47, & 18, 15, 16.
r ch. 12, 26. Deut. 6, 20. Josh. 4, 6, 21.
† Heb. *to-morrow*.
s ver. 3.
t ch. 12, 29.
u ver. 9.
x chap. 14, 11, 12. Numb. 14, 1-4.
y Deut. 17, 16.
z ch. 14, 2. Numb. 33, 6, &c.
|| Or, *by five in a rank*.

a Genesis 50, 25. Josh. 24, 32. Acts 7, 16.
b Numb. 33, 6.
c ch. 14, 19, 24, & 40, 38. Numb. 9, 15, & 10, 34, & 14, 14. Deut. 1, 33. Neh. 9, 12, 19. Ps. 78, 14, & 99, 7, & 105, 39. Isai. 4, 5. 1 Cor. 10, 1.

CHAPTER XIV.

1 God instructeth the Israelites in their journey. 5 Pharaoh pursueth after them. 10 The Israelites murmur. 13 Moses comforteth them. 15 God instructeth Moses. 19 The cloud removeth behind the camp. 21 The Israelites pass through the Red Sea, 23 which drowneth the Egyptians.

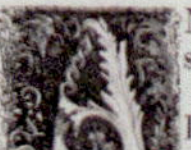

AND the LORD spake unto Moses, saying,
2 Speak unto the children of
Israel, [a]that they turn and en-
camp before [b]Pi-hahiroth, between [c]Migdol and the sea, over
against Baal-zephon: before it shall ye en-
camp by the sea.

a ch. 13, 18.
b Numb. 33, 7.
c Jer. 44, 1.

46. Illuminated Bible

NEW YORK: HARPER AND BROTHERS, 1846

2°: 844, 128, 356, 4, 8, 14, 34 p.; 340 mm. Hills 1161

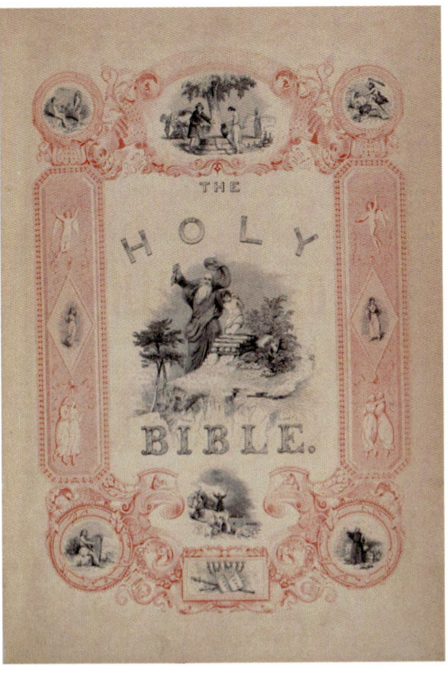

Fig. 46.1

Sturdier than any previous American edition of the King James text, the *Illuminated Bible* issued by the four Harper brothers in the early 1840s outclassed them all by the multitude and variety of its illustrations, the encyclopedic information of its scholarly apparatus, and the high quality of its printing. America's first illustrated Bible, printed by Isaiah Thomas in 1791 (Cat. 34), included 50 engravings and established a kind of unofficial canon most publishers felt compelled to adopt. In spectacular contrast with the common practice, the Harpers decided to publish a folio Bible that would include no fewer than "sixteen hundred historical engravings." Their new concept was supported by equally new technologies. In the United States, the Harpers were the first publishers to use powerful steam-run presses and the first to adopt electrotyping, a process developed in Europe in 1838. They installed steam presses in 1833 and first used electroplates to print their Bible. Electroplates are not unlike stereotype plates, but they have the huge advantage of allowing the printer to combine letterpress with illustrations on the same page and do not break when used in a steam press.

The publishing empire of the four Harper brothers started with a modest printing shop James (1795–1869) and John (1797–1875) opened in New York in 1817. In 1833 Joseph Wesley (1801–1870) and Fletcher (1806–1877) joined the firm, which changed its name from J. and J. Harper to Harper and Brothers. Over the decades the Harpers issued many popular books and a few less successful ones (*Moby Dick* was among them), a huge amount of textbooks and several magazines, but the *Illuminated Bible* remains their most important publication. The company survives as HarperCollins and is one of the leading publishers in the English-speaking world.

The Bible was more than three years in the making. In 1843 the Harpers opened a subscription list and announced the Bible would be published in 50 numbers available to the subscribers for 25 cents each. Their initial expenses were estimated at $25,000. The first number was probably released early in 1844 and the 54th and last one appeared in 1846. The press run for each number was 50,000 copies and an additional 25,000 copies[93] were printed and bound in hand-tooled morocco with gilt edges. Acclaimed by the press and enthusiastically purchased by the public, the edition sold out in a few years and was reprinted in 1858 or 1859. A second reprint followed in 1866.

The plates for the Harpers' Bible were executed by Joseph Alexander Adams (1803–1880), an American engraver who had experimented with the new technology since 1838 and was paid $60,000 for this project. The publishers commissioned original artwork from John Gadsby Chapman (1808–1889), a native of New Jersey, who executed some 1,400 designs. As suggested by the word *Illuminated* in the title of the Harpers' Bible, its overall decoration was meant to replicate the outlook of medieval biblical manuscripts. Starting in the early thirteenth century, handwritten copies of the Latin Bible usually displayed an ornamental initial at the beginning of each chapter. Adopting this practice in a printed edition of the King James Bible meant providing illustrations for 1,359 letters: 929 in the Old Testament, 170 in the Apocrypha, and 260 in the New Testament. Since the English alphabet has 26 letters and some of them are far more frequent than others, repeating the same design was both unavoidable and potentially annoying. Chapman showed his craftsmanship by creating multiple variants for the most common letters and skillfully alternating them. To balance the presence of decorative letters he also designed thumbnail images of persons or objects as a running visual commentary to the biblical text. Usually there are between three and five small images in two adjacent pages, but their number is occasionally as high as 13.

Chapman also designed 200 larger and more conventional illustrations that take about half a page each. Again he aimed for variety by creating elaborate borders for some of them while placing others in a sort of vacuum above the text. The Bible is open at Exodus 12–14 to show the way the illustrations and illuminated initials are combined with the text. Fig. 46.1 is a photograph of its engraved title page.

Abundantly provided with indexes, chronological tables, a concordance, and other scholarly paraphernalia, and embellished with unparalleled illustrations, the Harpers' *Illuminated Bible* was widely imitated by the countless Family Bibles published in the second half of the nineteenth century.[94]

8 ¶ And the Lord spake unto Moses and unto Aaron, saying,

9 When Pharaoh shall speak unto you, saying, Shew a miracle for you: then thou shalt say unto Aaron, Take thy rod, and cast *it* before Pharaoh, *and* it shall become a serpent.

10 ¶ And Moses and Aaron went in unto Pharaoh, and they did so as the Lord had commanded: and Aaron cast down his rod before Pharaoh, and before his servants, and it became a serpent.

11 Then Pharaoh also called the wise men and the sorcerers: now the magicians of Egypt, they also did in like manner with their enchantments.

12 For they cast down every man his rod, and they became serpents: but Aaron's rod swallowed up their rods.

13 And he hardened Pharaoh's heart, that he hearkened not unto them; as the Lord had said.

14 ¶ And the Lord said unto Moses, Pharaoh's heart *is* hardened, he refuseth to let the people go.

15 Get thee unto Pharaoh in the morning; lo, he goeth out unto the water; and thou shalt stand by the river's brink against he come; and the rod which was turned to a serpent shalt thou take in thine hand.

16 And thou shalt say unto him, The Lord God of the Hebrews hath sent me unto thee, saying, Let my people go, that they may serve me in the wilderness: and, behold, hitherto thou wouldest not hear.

17 Thus saith the Lord, In this thou shalt know that I *am* the Lord: behold, I will smite with the rod that *is* in mine hand upon the waters which *are* in the river, and they shall be turned to blood.

18 And the fish that *is* in the river shall die, and the river shall stink; and the Egyptians shall lothe to drink of the water of the river.

19 ¶ And the Lord spake unto Moses, Say unto Aaron, Take thy rod, and stretch out thine hand upon the waters of Egypt, upon their streams, upon their rivers, and upon their ponds, and upon all their pools of water, that they may become blood; and *that* there may be blood throughout all the land of Egypt, both in *vessels of* wood, and in *vessels of* stone.

20 And Moses and Aaron did so, as the Lord commanded; and he lifted up the rod, and smote the waters that *were* in the river, in the sight of Pharaoh, and in the sight of his servants; and all the waters that *were* in the river were turned to blood.

21 And the fish that *was* in the river died; and the river stank, and the Egyptians could not drink of the water of the river; and there was blood throughout all the land of Egypt.

22 And the magicians of Egypt did so with their enchantments: and Pharaoh's heart was hardened, neither did he hearken unto them; as the Lord had said.

23 And Pharaoh turned and went into his house, neither did he set his heart to this also.

24 And all the Egyptians digged round about the river for water to drink; for they could not drink of the water of the river.

25 And seven days were fulfilled, after that the Lord had smitten the river.

CHAPTER VIII.

1 Frogs are sent. 8 Pharaoh sueth to Moses, 12 and Moses by prayer removeth them away. 16 The dust is turned into lice, which the magicians would not do. 20 The swarms of flies. 25 Pharaoh inclineth to let the people go. 32 but yet is hardened.

AND the Lord spake unto Moses, Go unto Pharaoh, and say unto him, Thus saith the Lord, Let my people go, that they may serve me.

2 And if thou refuse to let *them* go, behold, I will smite all thy borders with frogs:

3 And the river shall bring forth frogs

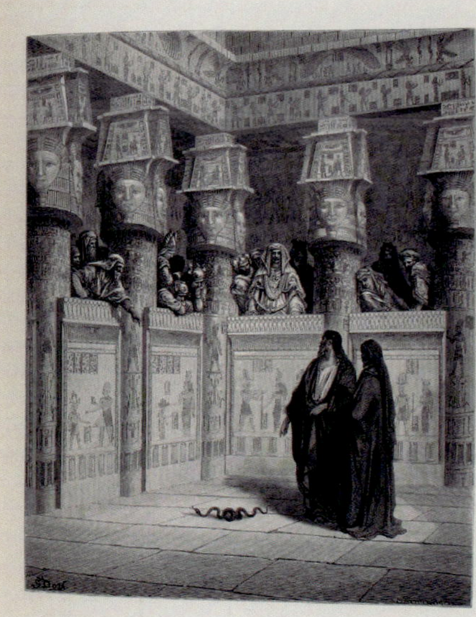

MOSES AND AARON BEFORE PHARAOH.

47. Bible with Apocrypha

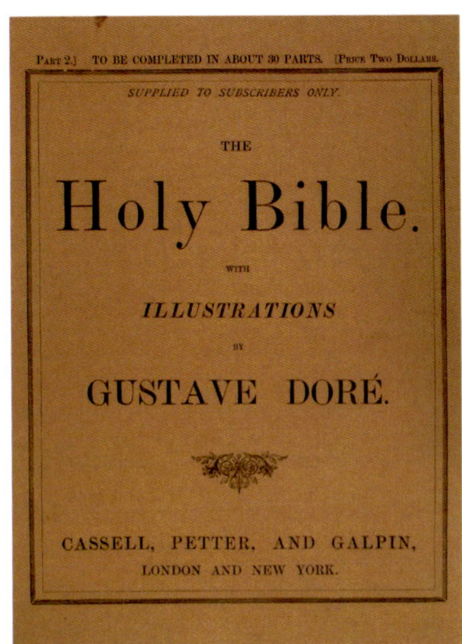

Fig. 47.1

In 1866, when 238 original drawings by Gustave Doré (1832–1883) were first used to embellish a Catholic version of the French Bible, the artist, though only in his thirties, had already established a solid reputation as a draftsman and book illustrator. He got his first commissions when he was only 15 and by the early 1860s he had created about 2,000 images to illustrate works by Cervantes, Dante, Shakespeare, and many others. His Bible illustrations earned him unparalleled international fame. Less than two years after the French version, Doré Bibles were also printed in English and German, and by the mid-1870s they were available in a dozen different languages.

Doré was extremely popular in England and the United States. He had his own gallery in London and his illustrations were included in almost all the Family Bibles printed in English on both sides of the Atlantic during the 1870s–1890s. They were also issued without the biblical text, in successive editions of the *Doré Bible Gallery* dating from the 1880s and 1890s and most recently reprinted in 2010. They became so much part of the popular culture that they found their way into one of the most successful films inspired by the Bible: Cecil B. DeMille's *Ten Commandments* (1923 and 1956).

The first English edition of the Doré Bible, although beautiful, is less spectacular than the French one. It is printed on slightly smaller paper and does not include the ornaments designed by Hector Giacomelli (1822–1904) for the French version. Doré's drawings suffered minor revisions when they were transferred from the French Catholic version to the Protestant King James Bible. In the Catholic tradition visual representations of God the Father are perfectly acceptable, but in many Protestant denominations they are not. Four of Doré's original drawings included a depiction of God the Father: the Creation of Light, the Formation of Eve, the Call of Abraham, and the Burning Bush. In the English edition, God's figure was erased from the first two images, and the last two were dropped altogether.

The Doré Bible was first issued in parts to subscribers and its price was $2 per number (see Fig 47.1). The bound edition is open to show the illustration facing Exodus 7–8.

THE

CAMBRIDGE PARAGRAPH BIBLE

OF THE

AUTHORIZED ENGLISH VERSION,

WITH THE TEXT REVISED BY A COLLATION OF ITS EARLY AND OTHER
PRINCIPAL EDITIONS,
THE USE OF THE ITALIC TYPE MADE UNIFORM,
THE MARGINAL REFERENCES REMODELLED,
AND A CRITICAL INTRODUCTION PREFIXED

BY

THE REV. F. H. SCRIVENER, M.A., LL.D.

RECTOR OF ST. GERRANS, EDITOR OF THE GREEK TESTAMENT, CODEX AUGIENSIS, &c.
ONE OF THE NEW TESTAMENT COMPANY OF REVISERS OF THE AUTHORIZED VERSION.

Edited for the Syndics of the University Press.

Cambridge:
AT THE UNIVERSITY PRESS.

———

LONDON: CAMBRIDGE WAREHOUSE, 17, PATERNOSTER ROW.
CAMBRIDGE: DEIGHTON, BELL AND CO.
1873.

[*All Rights reserved.*]

48. Cambridge Paragraph Bible

48. Cambridge
Paragraph Bible

CAMBRIDGE: UNIVERSITY PRESS, 1873
cxx, 856, 198, 253 p. 280 mm. Herbert 1995

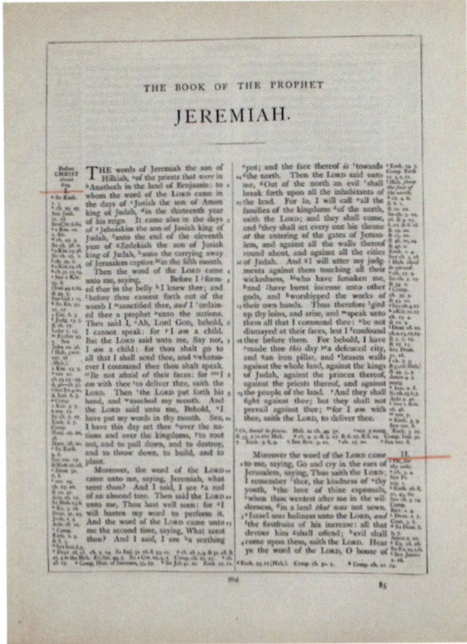

Fig. 48.1

As unofficial custodians of the King James Bible, the two British Universities had revised the 1611 text five times between 1629 and 1769, but ceased to make any new efforts in this area at the end of the 1760s. One hundred years later, the Syndics of Cambridge University Press entrusted to Frederick Henry Ambrose Scrivener (1813–1891) the task of preparing a new standard text of the King James Bible. Scrivener, who spent more than seven years laboring on the new edition, was well known for the important studies on the Greek text of the New Testament he had published between 1845 and 1864. Later on he would be a member of the British Committee who prepared the English Revised Version of the New Testament released in 1881.

As editor of the new Cambridge text of the 1611 Bible, Scrivener collated all its early or important editions, made uniform the use of the italic type, "remodeled" the marginal references, and wrote a comprehensive introduction that was reprinted in 1884 and is still read today.[95] He paid special attention to the graphic presentation of the text and broke up with the tradition that each biblical verse should start on a new line. The term *Paragraph* in the title of the 1873 edition refers to Scrivener's new division of the text into units of meaning that may combine several verses before ending in a line break. The chapter and verse numbers are relegated to the margins of the two columns and the distinction between biblical prose and biblical poetry is clearly indicated through the layout of the text. The Old Testament texts quoted in the New are printed in double-spaced letters in both Testaments.

Having painstakingly collated all the significant editions of the King James Bible, Scrivener was able to document the decisions he made when preparing his critical text. At the end of his preface he printed three lists that summarize the relations between the first two issues of the 1611 text (Cats. 16 and 17)[96] and his own text. The first one includes corrections to the 1611 text made in previous editions and accepted by Scrivener. This list runs for 19 dense pages in the 1873 edition and includes the date when each correction was first made. The second Appendix includes the variations that exist between the first two issues of the King James text

95. See the title page of the 1873 edition and Norton 2005: 122–125.

96. Herbert 309 and 319

and are unlikely to be simple printing errors. The last list contains corrections to the 1611 text made in previous editions and not accepted by Scrivener. While being duly impressed by Scrivener's thorough research, David Norton (see Cat. 52) feels he was wrong to take liberties with the Translators' text. He also considers that Scrivener did not go far enough in modernizing the spelling of the 1611 Bible.

The Bible is open at the title page. Fig 48.1 shows a sample text taken from the beginning of Jeremiah.

IN THE BEGINNING

GOD CREATED THE HEAVEN AND THE EARTH. ¶ AND THE EARTH WAS WITHOUT FORM, AND VOID; AND DARKNESS WAS UPON THE FACE OF THE DEEP, & THE SPIRIT OF GOD MOVED UPON THE FACE OF THE WATERS. ¶ And God said, Let there be light: & there was light. And God saw the light, that it was good: & God divided the light from the darkness. And God called the light Day, and the darkness he called Night. And the evening and the morning were the first day. ¶ And God said, Let there be a firmament in the midst of the waters, & let it divide the waters from the waters. And God made the firmament, and divided the waters which were under the firmament from the waters which were above the firmament: & it was so. And God called the firmament Heaven. And the evening & the morning were the second day. ¶ And God said, Let the waters under the heaven be gathered together unto one place, and let the dry land appear: and it was so. And God called the dry land Earth; and the gathering together of the waters called he Seas: and God saw that it was good. And God said, Let the earth bring forth grass, the herb yielding seed, and the fruit tree yielding fruit after his kind, whose seed is in itself, upon the earth: & it was so. And the earth brought forth grass, & herb yielding seed after his kind, & the tree yielding fruit, whose seed was in itself, after his kind: and God saw that it was good. And the evening & the morning were the third day. ¶ And God said, Let there be lights in the firmament of the heaven to divide the day from the night; and let them be for signs, and for seasons, and for days, & years: and let them be for lights in the firmament of the heaven to give light upon the earth: & it was so. And God made two great lights; the greater light to rule the day, and the lesser light to rule the night: he made the stars also. And God set them in the firmament of the heaven to give light upon the earth, and to rule over the day and over the night, & to divide the light from the darkness: and God saw that it was good. And the evening and the morning were the fourth day. ¶ And God said, Let the waters bring forth abundantly the moving creature that hath life, and fowl that may fly above the earth in the open firmament of heaven. And God created great whales, & every living creature that moveth, which the waters brought forth abundantly, after their kind, & every winged fowl after his kind: & God saw that it was good. And God blessed them, saying, Be fruitful, & multiply, and fill the waters in the seas, and let fowl multiply in the earth. And the evening & the morning were the fifth day. ¶ And God said, Let the earth bring forth the living creature after his kind, cattle, and creeping thing, and beast of the earth after his kind: and it was so. And God made the beast of the earth after his kind, and cattle after their kind, and every thing that creepeth upon the

49. Bible with Apocrypha

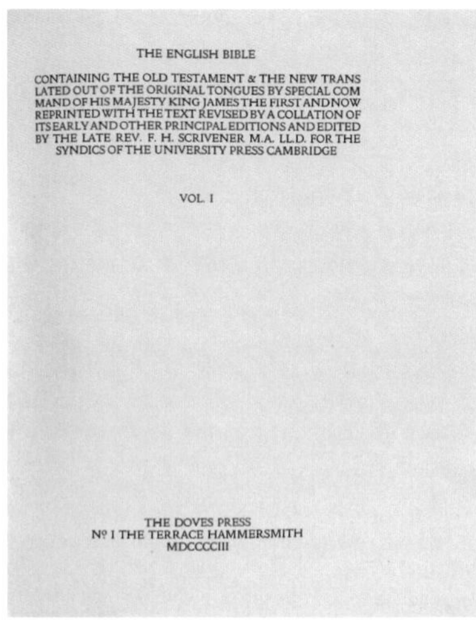

Fig. 48.1

Located in Hammersmith in west London and named after a neighboring pub, the Doves Press produced a variety of bibliophile editions between 1900 and 1909 under the joint direction of Thomas James Cobden-Sanderson (1840–1922) and Emery Walker (1851–1933). Cobden-Sanderson had founded the very successful Doves Bindery and Walker had helped William Morris (1834–1896) design his famous types. Their professional relationship was stormy; their partnership was dissolved in 1909. The Bible they produced took about three years to print.[97] Like all the books issued by the Doves Press between 1900 and 1909 it

97. Tidcombe 2003: 42–46

was printed from a new type commissioned by Cobden-Sanderson and executed by the punch cutter Edward P. Prince (1846–1923) under the supervision of Walker. The type was modeled upon the font used by Nicolas Jenson in the 1470s and was produced in one size. In about 1917, Cobden-Sanderson ensured that no Doves Press books would be printed after his death by throwing into the Thames all the type, the matrices, and the punches. Unlike his partner, Cobden-Sanderson made a point of always acknowledging the work of all persons involved in producing his books and included in the colophons of the Bible a list of compositors and pressmen.

As indicated in the title page, the biblical text published by the two associates is reprinted from the *Cambridge Paragraph Bible* edited by F. H. A. Scrivener in 1873 (Cat. 48). Cobden-Sanderson, who served as editor of the Doves Bible, dropped all the notes and references included in the Cambridge edition and printed a bare text preceded by the original preface and completed by the dedication to King James, placed as a sort of appendix after the end of Revelation. The Doves Bible is strikingly designed as a succession of compact pages filled with text from the left end of the first line to the right end of the last one. The chapter numbers are relegated to the margins and there are no verse numbers whatsoever. The indents that marked the division into paragraphs performed by Scrivener are replaced in the Doves Bible by a beautiful paragraph sign copied from the 1611 edition. There is, however, a distinction between prose and poetry in the Doves Bible. As is customary, the poetic texts of the Bible are printed in short lines and were divided into stanzas by Cobden-Sanderson himself. Fig 49.1 shows the title page of its first volume.

GOD

IN THE BEGINNING GOD CREATED THE HEAVEN AND THE EARTH. AND THE EARTH WAS WITHOUT FORM, AND VOID; AND DARKNESS WAS UPON THE FACE OF THE DEEP. AND THE SPIRIT OF GOD MOVED UPON THE FACE OF THE WATERS. AND GOD SAID, LET THERE BE LIGHT: AND THERE WAS LIGHT. AND GOD SAW THE LIGHT, THAT IT WAS GOOD: AND GOD DIVIDED THE LIGHT FROM THE DARKNESS. AND GOD CALLED THE LIGHT DAY, AND THE DARKNESS HE CALLED NIGHT. AND THE EVENING AND THE MORNING WERE THE FIRST DAY. ☾ AND GOD SAID, LET THERE BE A FIRMAMENT IN THE MIDST OF THE WATERS, AND LET IT DIVIDE THE WATERS FROM THE WATERS.

And God made the firmament, and divided the waters which were under the firmament from the waters which were above the firmament: and it was so. And God called the firmament Heaven. And the evening and the morning were the second day. ☾ And God said, Let the waters under the heaven be gathered together unto one place, and let the dry land appear: and it was so. And God called the dry land Earth; and the gathering together of the waters called he Seas: and God saw that it was good. And God said, Let the earth bring forth grass, the herb yielding seed, and the fruit tree yielding fruit after his kind, whose seed is in itself, upon the earth: and it was so. And the earth brought forth grass, and herb yielding seed after his kind, and the tree yielding fruit, whose seed was in itself, after his kind: and God saw that it was good. And the evening and the morning were the third day. ☾ And God said, Let there be lights in the firmament of the heaven to divide the day from the night; and let them be for signs, and for seasons, and for days, and years: And let them be for lights in the firmament of the heaven to give light upon the earth: and it was so. And God made two great lights; the greater light to rule the day, and the lesser light to rule the night: he made the stars also. And God set them in the firmament of the heaven to give light upon the earth, And to rule over the day and over the night, and to divide the light from the darkness: and God saw that it was good. And the evening and the morning were the fourth day. And God said, Let the waters bring forth abundantly the moving creature that hath life, and fowl that may fly above the earth in the open firmament of heaven. And God created great whales, and every living creature that moveth, which the waters brought forth abundantly, after their kind, and every winged fowl after his kind: and God saw that it was good. And God blessed them, saying, Be fruitful, and multiply, and fill the waters in the seas, and let fowl multiply in the earth. And the evening and the morning were the fifth day. ☾ And God said, Let the earth bring forth the living creature after his kind, cattle, and creeping thing, and beast of the earth after his kind: and it was so. And God made the beast of the earth after his kind, and cattle after their kind, and every thing that creepeth upon the earth after his kind: and God saw that it was good.

51. Bible

51. Bible | North Hatfield, Mass. and New York: Pennyroyal Caxton Press, 1999

2 vols.: 187, 247, 109 p.; 197, 234 p. 229 ill. 410 mm.

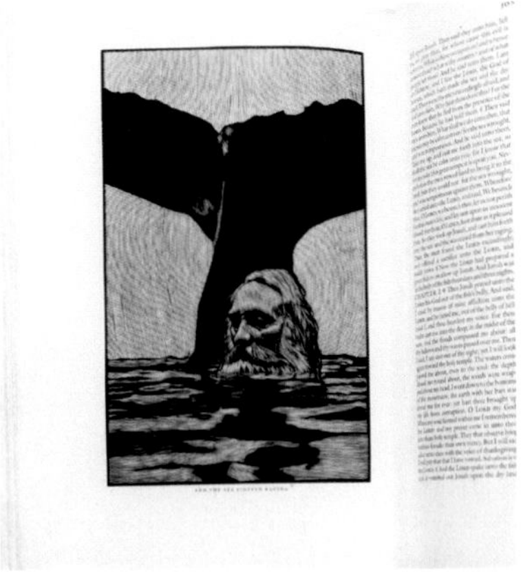

Fig. 51.1

Advertised as a publishing event of true millennial significance and released in the last quarter of 1999, the Pennyroyal Caxton Press Bible has earned a privileged place among the most beautifully printed editions of the King James text and is often compared to the Bibles produced by John Baskerville in 1763 and the Doves Press and Bruce Rogers in the twentieth century. It was both designed and illustrated by Barry Moser (b. 1940), a multitalented artist with vast experience as a printer, painter and printmaker. Moser was the first major artist to create a complete set of Bible illustrations for a folio volume since Gustave Doré had done it in the 1860s.

Like the Doves Press and Bruce Rogers before him, Barry Moser reprinted the text of the 1873 *Cambridge Parallel Bible* edited by F. H. A. Scrivener (see Cat. 48) and jettisoned all editorial additions, including the verse numbering. Unlike them, he omitted the Apocrypha. Moser made a point of creating at least one image for each of the 66 books of the Old and New Testaments including the shortest ones. Intensely personal and often provocative, his images tend to depict people rather than events, landscapes or large scenes.[98]

98. See Madsen 2000

In the making of the 1999 Bible traditional techniques and materials were combined with cutting edge technology and expertise. The folio Bible was printed on handmade paper from computer-generated type. The red initials at the beginning of each book were drawn by hand as were the words *God, Christ,* and *Amen* that mark the beginning of the Old and New Testaments and the end of the Bible. The original images created by Barry Moser were engraved not in wood, but in a polymer resin that replicates the texture of the nearly unobtainable hardwood.

In addition to the 400 copies of this limited edition, the publishers also produced a reasonably priced commercial edition that sold 50,000 in two weeks.

The Bible is open at the beginning of Genesis. Fig 51.1 is a photograph of the image Moser created to illustrate the Book of Jonah.

THE BOOK OF THE PROPHET
JEREMIAH

1 The words of Jeremiah the son of Hilkiah, of the priests that were in Anathoth in the land of Benjamin: ²to whom the word of the LORD came in the days of Josiah the son of Amon king of Judah, in the thirteenth year of his reign. ³It came also in the days of Jehoiakim the son of Josiah king of Judah, unto the end of the eleventh year of Zedekiah the son of Josiah king of Judah, unto the carrying away of Jerusalem captive in the fifth month.

⁴Then the word of the LORD came unto me, saying,

⁵ 'Before I formed thee in the belly I knew thee;
and before thou camest forth out of the womb I sanctified thee,
and I ordained thee a prophet unto the nations'.

⁶Then said I, 'Ah, Lord GOD, behold, I cannot speak: for I am a child'. ⁷But the LORD said unto me, 'Say not, "I am a child": for thou shalt go to all that I shall send thee, and whatsoever I command thee thou shalt speak. ⁸Be not afraid of their faces: for I am with thee to deliver thee,' saith the LORD. ⁹Then the LORD put forth his hand, and touched my mouth, and the LORD said unto me, 'Behold, I have put my words in thy mouth. ¹⁰See, I have this day set thee over the nations and over the kingdoms, to root out, and to pull down, and to destroy, and to throw down, to build, and to plant.'

¹¹Moreover the word of the LORD came unto me, saying, 'Jeremiah, what seest thou?' And I said, 'I see a rod of an almond tree'. ¹²Then said the LORD unto me, 'Thou hast well seen: for I will hasten my word to perform it'.

¹³And the word of the LORD came unto me the second time, saying, 'What seest thou?' And I said, 'I see a seething pot'; and the face thereof was towards the north. ¹⁴Then the LORD said unto me, 'Out of the north an evil shall break forth upon all the inhabitants of the land. ¹⁵For lo, I will call all the families of the kingdoms of the north,' saith the LORD, 'and they shall come, and they shall set every one his throne at the entering of the gates of Jerusalem, and against all the walls thereof round about, and against all the cities of Judah. ¹⁶And I will utter my judgements against them touching all their wickedness, who have forsaken me, and have burnt incense unto other gods, and worshipped the works of their own hands.

¹⁷'Thou therefore gird up thy loins, and arise, and speak unto them all that I command thee: be not dismayed at their faces, lest I confound thee before them. ¹⁸For behold, I have made thee this day a defenced city, and an iron pillar, and brazen walls against the whole land, against the kings of Judah, against the princes thereof, against the priests thereof, and against the people of the land. ¹⁹And they shall

52. New Cambridge Paragraph Bible

CAMBRIDGE: UNIVERSITY PRESS, 2005

xxxvi, 1868 p. 270 mm.

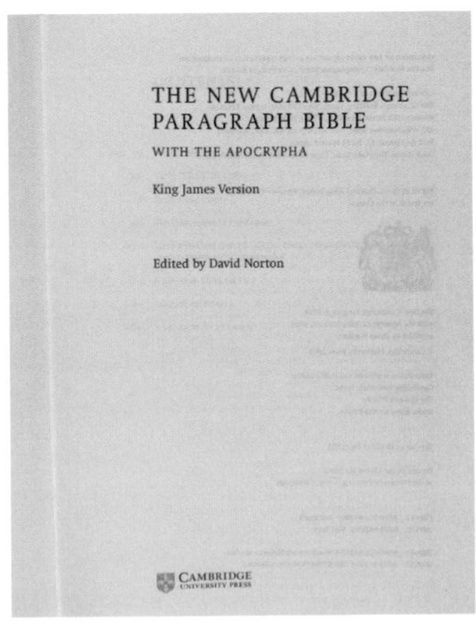

Fig. 52.1

In 1994 Cambridge University Press had to replace the film used to print its King James Bibles and decided to update the electronic files of its standard text. Initially the publisher considered revamping the *Cambridge Paragraph Bible* edited by F. H. A. Scrivener in 1873 (see Cat. 48) and collated it against the current standard text. The final decision was to commission a new text and the task of editing it was entrusted to David Norton, the author of an important monograph on the English Bible as literature first published in 1993 and a scholar of international stature. Norton's approach was both conservative and revisionist. His aim was to identify the Translators' text based on the 1611 first edition and the recently discovered manuscripts that document their work and to present it to the public in modernized spelling and attractive format. Norton limited his textual corrections to obvious typographical errors in the 1611 edition and refused to interfere with the Translators' choices in order to bring their version closer to the original Hebrew and Greek texts. In updating the spelling he made more changes than any previous editor, but did not attempt to alter grammatical forms. He unified variants such as *spoke* and *spake,* which he considered random orthographic alternatives, but did not change *thou wouldst* into *you would.*

In the layout of the pages, Norton adopted the paragraph format first used by Scrivener, but did not always conform to his predecessor's way of dividing the text. He kept the verse numbering and the marginal notes, but discarded the chapter summaries and the italics. Most importantly, he reprinted Miles Smith's original preface in modernized spelling and with updated footnotes. The Bible is open at the beginning of Jeremiah. Fig. 52.1 is a photograph of its title page.

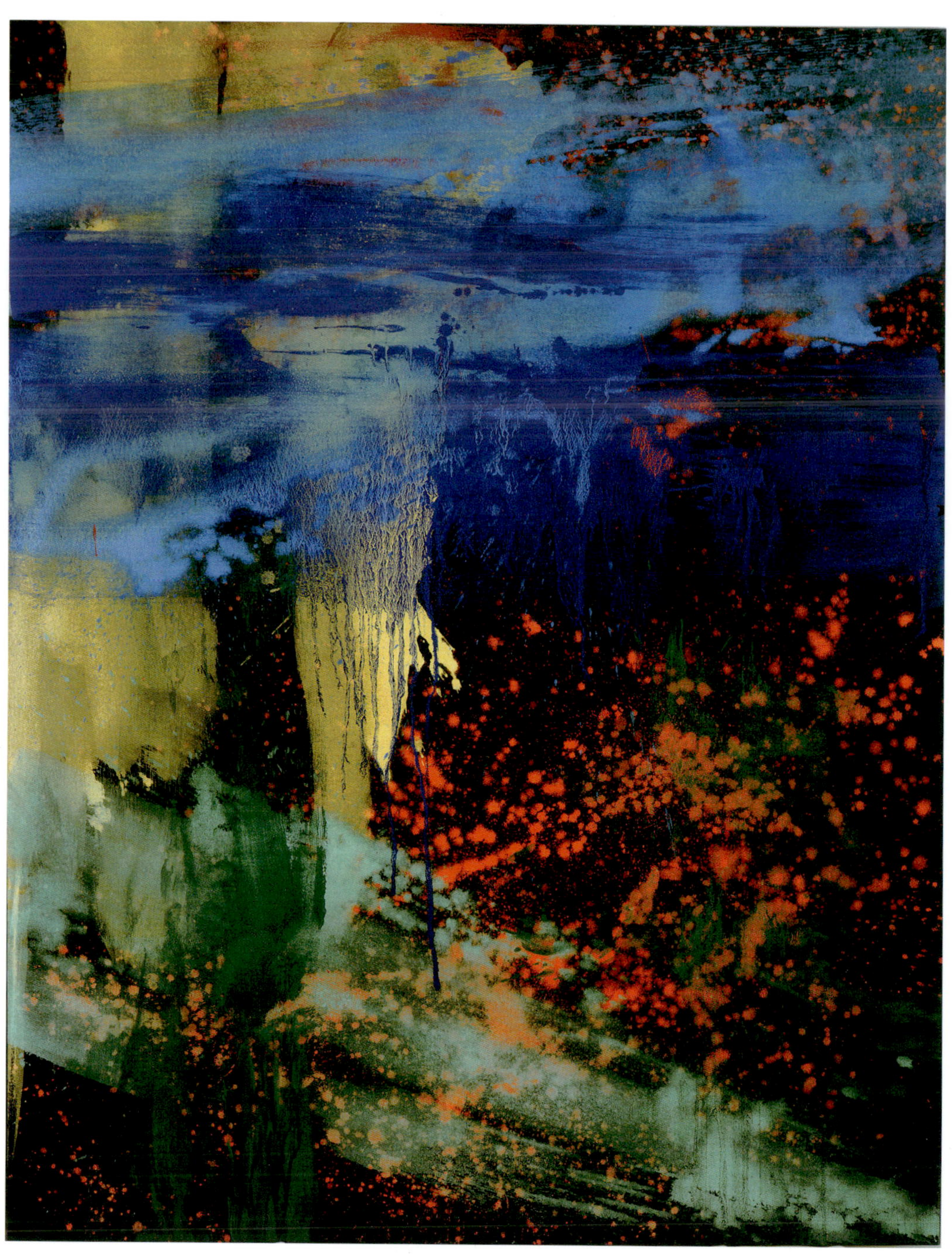

53. Charis–Kairos (Tears of Christ)

VII. Celebrating the King James Bible in 2011

MAKOTO FUJIMURA'S *THE FOUR HOLY GOSPELS*

Makoto Fujimura's visual interpretation of the Bible is well-suited to a twenty-first century audience. Created to commemorate the four hundredth anniversary of the King James Bible, and commissioned for publication by Crossway, *The Four Holy Gospels* is unique among illuminated biblical manuscripts for its lack of traditional representational imagery. Instead, the artist uses his signature abstractions to convey the resonance of the Bible in the contemporary world. Though informed by such twentieth century artists as Georges Rouault and Mark Rothko, Fujimura undertook this project in part to fill the void he detected in biblically inspired illuminations in twentieth century art. Fujimura states: "In taking on this project, it is my bold and ambitious prayer that this new century will see a re-visitation of the illuminated legacy, with the Bible as a source of creative inspiration and artistic expression, in both the East and the West."

Exhibited here are five large-scale frontispieces, one for each Gospel—Matthew, Mark, Luke and John—and one symbolizing the tears of Christ, as well as 89 letters, the opening letter of each chapter of each Gospel. The artist constructs his paintings layer upon layer using Japanese materials and pigments made of ground precious minerals. The compositions are also often hand-touched with gold or platinum.

In transcending the purely literary aspects of the Bible, Fujimura's paintings achieve universality and adhere to his belief in "the greater reality that the Bible speaks of…"

Adrianne Rubin, Ph.D.
Assistant Curator/Registrar

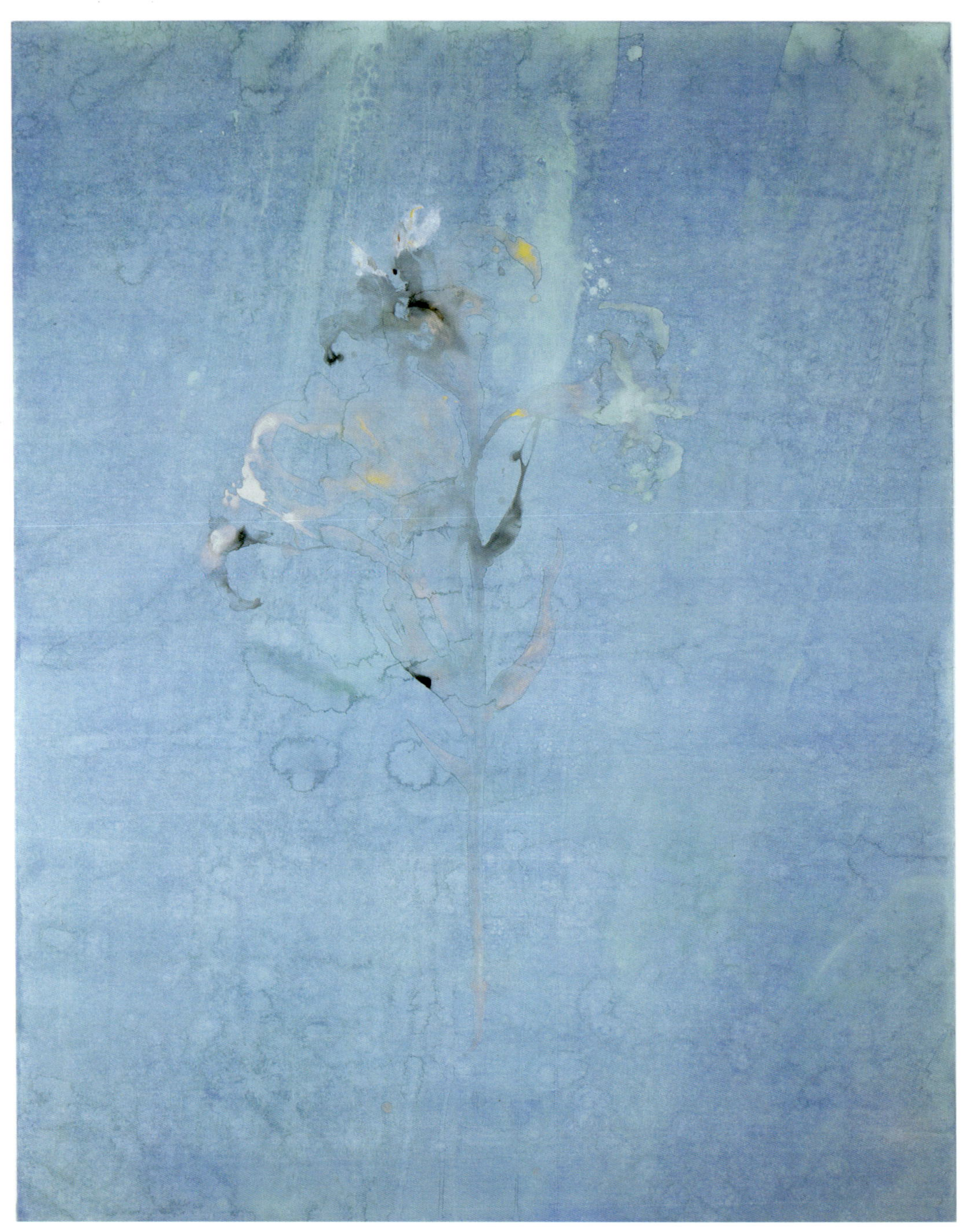

54. Matthew — Consider the Lilies

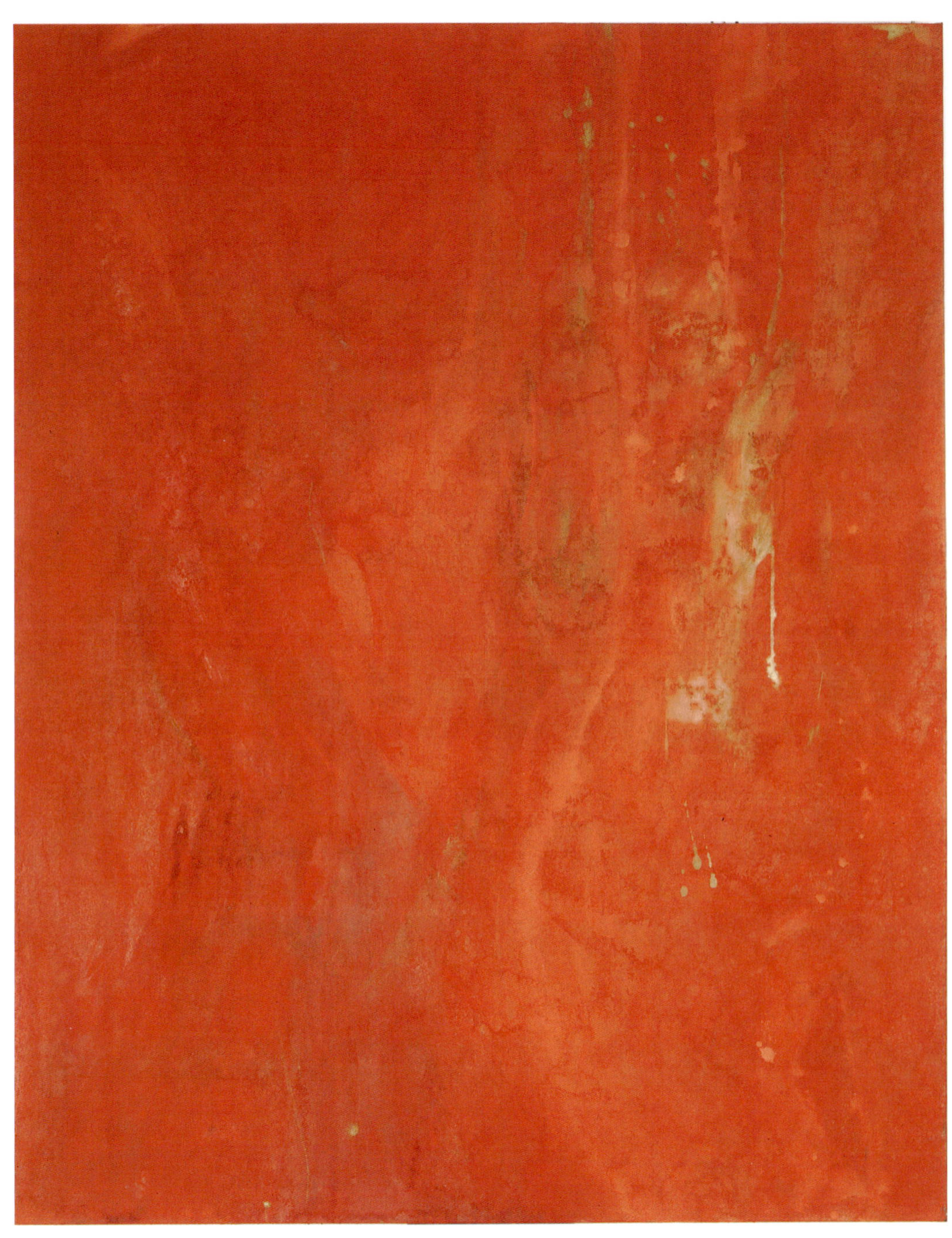

55. Mark — Water Flames

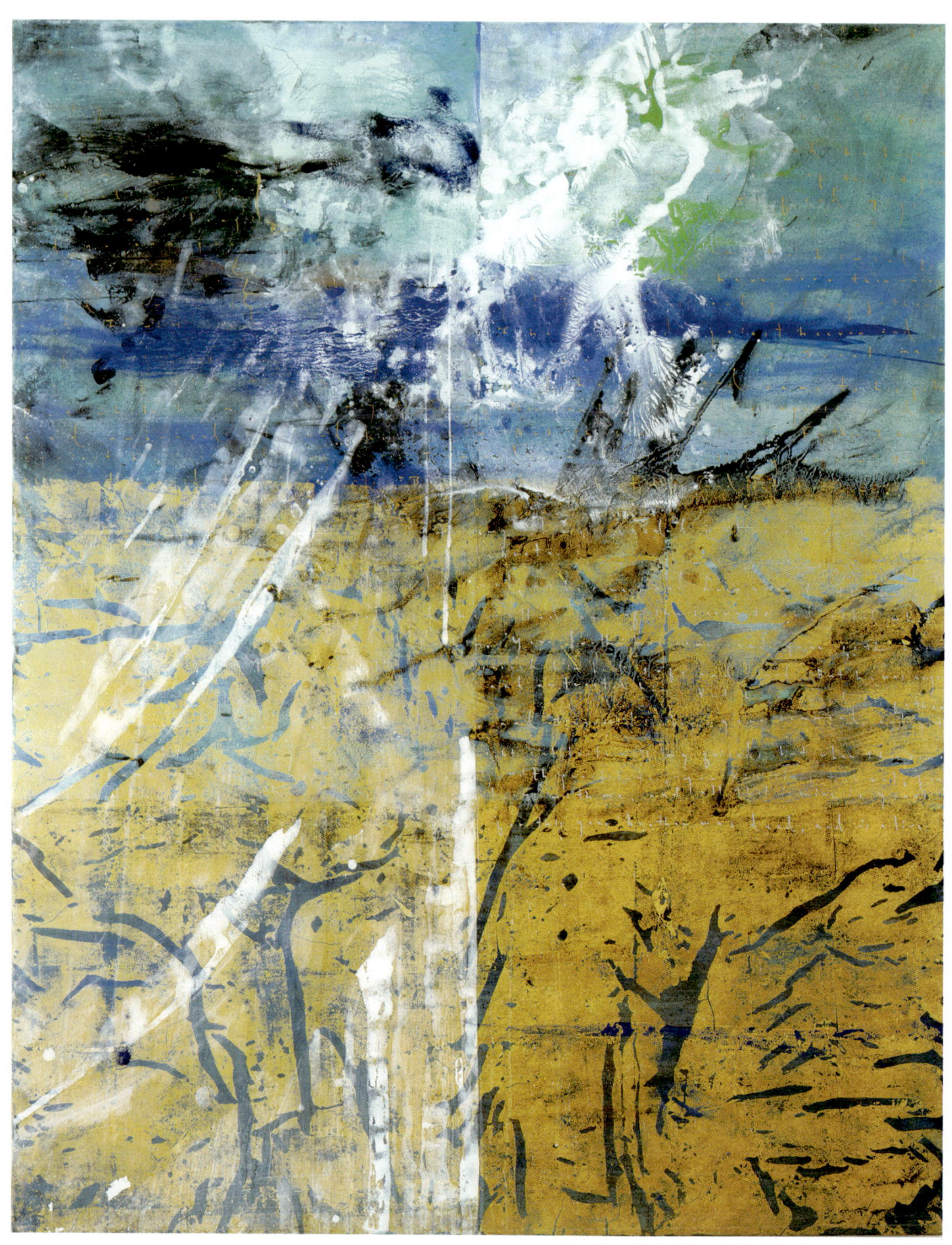

56. Luke — Prodigal God

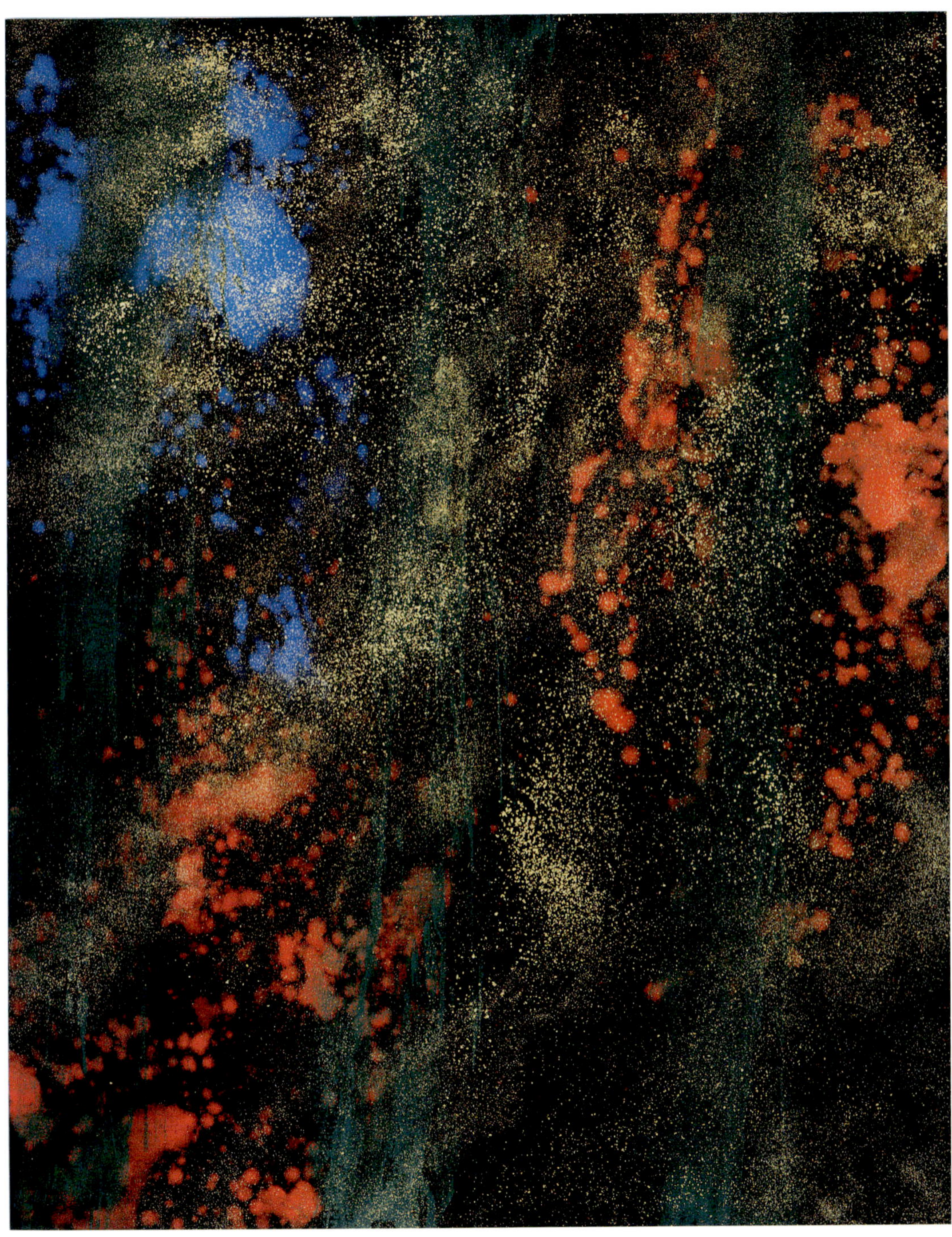

57. John—In the Beginning

I. The English Bible before King James

1. New Testament. *Wyclif version*
    Manuscript on vellum, ca. 1440

2. New Testament. *Tyndale version*
    [Worms: Peter Schoeffer, 1526]
    Facsimile edition, London: Paradine,
    1976

3. Pentateuch. *Tyndale version*
    [Antwerp: Johannes Hoochstraten],
    1530

4. Bible with Apocrypha. *Coverdale
    version*
    [Marburg?: E. Cervicornus and J.
    Soter?], 1535

5. Bible with Apocrypha. *Matthew's
    version*
    [Antwerp: R. Grafton and E.
    Whitchurch], 1537

6. Bible with Apocrypha. *Great Bible
    version*
    [London]: Richard Grafton and Edward
    Whitchurch, 1539

7. Bible with Apocrypha. *Geneva version*
    Geneva: Rowland Hall, 1560

8. Bible with Apocrypha. *Bishops' version*
    London: Richard Jugge, 1568

9. New Testament. *Rheims-Douay version*
    Rheims: John Fogny, 1582

10. Old Testament with Apocrypha.
    Rheims-Douay version
    Douay: Laurence Kellam, 1609–1610

II. Birth of a Masterpiece

11. William Barlow (d. 1613)
    *The Summe and Substance of the
    Conference … at Hampton Court*
    [London: Printed by John Windet
    for Mathew Law, 1604]
    Facsimile edition Gainesville, FL:
    Scholars' Facsimile and Reprints, 1965

12. Metrical Psalms in English
    Oxford: William Turner, 1631

13. Bible with Apocrypha. *Bishops' version*
    London: Robert Barker, 1602

14. Hebrew Bible
    Venice: Daniel Bomberg, 1524–25
    V. 2 (Joshua, Judges, 1–2 Samuel, 1–2
    Kings) 21 November 1524

15. New Testament in Greek and Latin
    [Geneva]: Heirs of Eustache Vignon,
    1598

1. Portrait of King James
    Oil on canvas by Daniel Mytens, 1621
    148.6 x 100.6 cm.
    National Portrait Gallery, London

2. Portrait of John Reynolds
    Line engraving by Magdalena de Passe or Willem de Passe, 1620
    168 x 128 mm.
    National Portrait Gallery, London

3. Portrait of Richard Bancroft
    Line engraving by George Vertue, 1745
    187 x 118 mm.
    National Portrait Gallery, London

4. Portrait of Lancelot Andrewes
    Line engraving by Simon de Passe, 1618
    177 x 107 mm.
    National Portrait Gallery, London

5. Portrait of John Bois
    Engraved title page of Bois' collected works, London: William Ashley, 1622
    267 x 169 mm.
    National Portrait Gallery, London

6. Lists of Translators
    British Library, Ms. Harley 750 fol. 1 r

7. Rules for Translating
    British Library, Ms. Harley 750 fol. 1v

8, 8.1. John Bois' Notes to Romans 1:9 to 6:22
    Oxford, Corpus Christi College, Ms. CCC 312 fol. 61

1. *Catalogs and Bibliographies*

DM
Darlow, T. H. and H.F. Moule. *Historical Catalogue of the Printed Editions of Holy Scripture, in the Library of the British and Foreign Bible Society.* Vol. II London: BFBS, 1911

Herbert
Historical Catalogue of the Printed Editions of the English Bible, 1535–1961. Revised and expanded ... by A.S. Herbert. London and New York: British and Foreign Bible Society and American Bible Society, 1968

Hills
Margaret T. Hills. *The English Bible in America.* New York: American Bible Society and The New York Public Library, 1961

WLB
Württembergische Landesbibliothek. *Bibelsammlung der Württembergischen Landesbibliothek.* Stuttgart-Bad Cannstatt: Fromann-Holzboog, 1984–

2. *General Works*

Allen, Ward (editor and translator). *Translating for King James.* Nashville, TN: Vanderbilt University Press, 1969

American Bible Society. Committee on Versions. *Report on the History and Recent Collation of the English Version of the Bible.* New York: American bible Society, 1851

Burke, David G. (editor). *Translation that Openeth the Window.* Atlanta: Society of Biblical Literature, 2009

Canton, William. *History of the British and Foreign Bible Society.* 4 vols. London: Murray 1904

Carleton, James G. *The Part of Rheims in the Making of the English Bible.* Oxford: Clarendon Press, 1902

Chambers, Bettye Thomas. *Bibliographie of French Bibles. Fifteenth and Sixteenth centuries.* Geneva: Droz, 1983

Daniell, David (editor). *Tyndale's Old Testament.* New Haven and London: Yale University Press, 1992

Daniell, David. *The Bible in English.* New Haven and London: Yale University Press, 2003

De Hamel, Christopher. *The Book: a history of the Bible.* London: Phaidon, 2001

Dobson, William T. *History of the Bassandyne Bible.* Edinburgh: Blackwood, 1887

Exman, Eugene. *The Brothers Harper.* New York: Harper and Row, 1965

Exman, Eugene. *The House of Harper.* New York: Harper and Row, 1967

Gutjahr, Paul C. *An American Bible.* Stanford : Stanford University Press, 1999

Hills, Margaret T. *Production and Supply of Scriptures, 1831–1860.* "ABS Historical Essays 18., Part III. November, 1964

Hixson, Richard F. *Isaac Collins: a Quaker printer in 18th Century America.* New Brunswick, NJ: Rutgers University Press, 1968

Lattré, Guido. *The 1535 Coverdale Bible and its Antwerp origins.* In: Orlaith O'Sullivan and Ellen N. Herron editors. *The Bible as Book: the Reformation.* New Castle, Del.: Oak Knoll, 2000

Madsen, Catherine. "A Terrible Beauty: Moser's Bible." In: *Cross Currents* vol. 50. 1–2, 2000

McKerrow, R. B. (General Editor). *Dictionary of Printers and Booksellers in England, Scotland and Ireland, and of Foreign Printers of English Books (1557–1640).* London: Bibliographical Society, 1968 (1910)

McMullin, B.J. *The 1629 Cambridge Bible.* In *Transactons and Proceedings of the Cambridge Bibliographical Society* 8.4 (1984), p. 381–397

Mozley, J.F. *Coverdale and his Bibles.* London: Lutterworth, 1953

Nicolson, Adam. *God's Secretaries.* New York: HarperCollins, 2003

Norton, David. *History of the English Bible as Literature.* Cambridge; University Press, 2000

Norton, David. *A Textual History of the King James Bible.* Cambridge: University Press, 2005

O'Callaghan, Edmund Bailey. *A List of Editions of the Holy Scriptures ... printed in America previous to 1860.* Albany: Munsell and Rowland, 1861

Opfell, Olga S. *The King James Bible Translators.* Jefferson and London: McFarland, 1982

Payne, Gustavus S. *The Men Behind the King James Version.* Grand Rapids, MI: Baker, 1959 (1977)

Pollard, Alfred W. *Records of the English Bible, the documents relating to the translation and publication of the Bible in English, 1525–1611.* London, New York: H. Frowde, Oxford University Press, 1911. Also included in the facsimile edition published by Oxford University Press in 1911 (Herbert 2166)

Tidcombe, Marianne. *The Doves Press.* New Castle, DE: Oak Knoll Press, 2003

Willoughby, Edwin E. *The Making of the King James Bible* Los Angeles: Printed for Dawson's Book Shop at the Plantin Press, 1956

Wright, John. *Early Bibles of America.* New York: Thomas Whittaker, 1894